Boadilla

By the same author:

OUT OF BOUNDS
(*in collaboration with Giles Romilly*)

Esmond Romilly

Boadilla

With an introduction and notes
by Hugh Thomas

Macdonald · London

First published in 1937 by Hamish Hamilton
Published in 1971 by
Macdonald & Co. (Publishers) Ltd,
St Giles House, 49/50 Poland Street,
London W.1

SBN 356 03534 4
Printed in Great Britain by
Tonbridge Printers Ltd
Peach Hall Works, Tonbridge, Kent

In Memory of

Harry Addley   Sidney Avener

Lorrimer Birch   Raymond Cox   James W. Gough

Arnold Jeans   Martin Messer

*Members of the Thaelmann Battallion of
the Spanish Republican Army, killed in
action at Boadilla del Monte on
20 December* 1936

Introduction to the new edition

Boadilla del Monte is a small poor Castillian village (population about a thousand) about fifteen miles from Madrid. Even today, it is still poor and very far from 'civilization': a purely agricultural village, it is scarcely believable that it is so short a distance from the capital. In 1936, it was the scene of a brief but disastrous skirmish, in the course of which most of the English contingent in the recently constituted International Brigade were killed, fighting on behalf of the Spanish Republic against General Franco.

Among the two survivors of this encounter was Esmond Romilly (the other survivor, Bert Ovenden, was killed a few months later in the big battle of Brunete, which by chance took place about five miles to the west, around an if anything even poorer village). Esmond Romilly was a brilliant and attractive rebel who was then aged eighteen. He was the son of a soldier who had fought with great distinction in the First World War, and his mother was sister to Mrs Winston Churchill. He had run away from Wellington College aged fifteen and, on his own, founded a newspaper, *Out of Bounds*, dedicated to inculcating revolution in public schools. His brief life has been already luminously described, first by his best friend, Philip Toynbee, in *Friends Apart* (MacGibbon and Kee, 1954) and more recently by his widow, Jessica Mitford, in *Hons and Rebels* (Gollancz, 1960). So this new edition of his account of his months fighting in Spain to which he gave the name of the last engagement does not need much more personal comment, save to recall that, as *Hons and Rebels* makes clear, *Boadilla* was begun by its author in the Hotel des Basques at Saint Jean de Luz in the spring of 1937. Romilly had left Spain after the battle described in the book and returned to England. He then eloped with Jessica Mitford and went as an unofficial reporter to the then briefly autonomous Basque Republic. After British Government intervention on behalf of Miss Mitford (who had been made a ward of court by her parents) and after the beginning of Franco's Basque campaign, Romilly had moved back to France. After some weeks, Romilly and Miss Mitford were married, with the final if still most reluctant approval of the latter's parents. At some stage soon after he secured an advance of £50 from the publishers (Hamish Hamilton) which 'undreamed of' wealth was soon gambled away at the *Boule* table at Dieppe in an unsuccessful attempt to secure a fortune. The book was published in October 1937. Romilly was then nineteen.

The book belongs, as the reader will see, to the heroic period of the Spanish Civil War, both in respect of what actually happened and how it seemed to the participants. There are, it is true, descriptions of the unpreparedness and incompetence of the Republican army and impressions of war disillusion. We are reminded that war is as much a question of cleaning and making lists as of glory, while the passages where Romilly described his unsuccessful attempts to discover what was happening in the middle of what figures in books as a pitched battle would have satisfied Tolstoy. On the other hand, Romilly has no doubt whatever that he is fighting fascism and that Madrid might be the 'grave of European fascism'. Nor does he lay special emphasis upon any serious divisions between the different elements in the Republican camp, in particular those between the communists on the one side and the anarchists on the other. Disillusion with communist methods was, without doubt, one reason for the Republican defeat. After Romilly had left Spain, these divisions burst out into actual fighting and the war in Spain might very well not have ended as it did had it not been for an open civil war within the civil war in the heart of the exhausted Republican camp, in the spring of 1939. All this was for the future. So too were the serious dissensions which sprang up even within the International Brigades from the beginning of 1937.

Boadilla is an account of Romilly's life with the English volunteers for Spain between sometime in October 1936 and December of the same year. During this period, he and his unit were involved in three engagements: one at Cerro de los Angeles, to the south of Madrid, in early November; one in the University City, or rather in one of the innumerable side actions which constituted that memorable street battle; and finally, at Boadilla del Monte, a village to the north-west of Madrid. All these clashes were part of the long battle for Madrid which lasted the winter of 1936–7. General Franco's forces, advancing on the capital from the south and west, sought first to take the city by assault. Beaten back in the University City, Franco then tried to surround the city. Here too, after the famous battle of Guadalajara in late February 1937 (which Hemingway described with some over-enthusiasm as one of the decisive battles of the world), Franco's forces were held up. The attempt to capture Madrid was abandoned and another offensive was launched by the Spanish White armies (or the insurgents, or the rebels, or the nationalists, as they were varyingly known), at first on the Republican redoubts in the Basque provinces, afterwards on Aragón and Catalonia. Madrid was never really conquered in battle; it was in the end surrendered without a fight.

In this famous battle of Madrid in 1936–7, the International Brigades clearly played a considerable part. Exactly how great a part is naturally a controversial matter. The appearance of well-disciplined foreign troops in the streets of Madrid, and the well managed publicity surrounding that event, evidently gave a great boost to the morale of the city, and obviously morale plays if anything a greater part in civil wars than national conflicts. The actual example of the foreign volunteers, in particular the German communists, in the fighting itself was elevating to their Spanish comrades, and there is something to be said for the argument that the arrival of these superior troops, in the nick of time, when Madrid was everywhere expected to fall, and when the Government had left the city for Valencia, was decisive. Would the battles in the University City have been won without the International Brigades? It is doubtful. The same doubts exist over the role of the brigades in the prolonged fighting along the Madrid–Corunna road (of which the battle of Boadilla was an offshoot) and at Guadalajara.

There is now no secret about the manner of organization of the Brigades. When the Spanish War began, many people in northern Europe thought, with Stephen Spender, that 'at last the gloves were off in the struggle against Fascism.' In late July and August therefore a motley collection of idealists and adventurers headed for Spain. Prominent among these were exiles from Germany and Italy, or from other right-wing regimes in central or east Europe. Most of these early volunteers travelled, as Romilly did, on their own initiative, expecting to find in Spain the European civil war that had in some way failed to break out in their own countries; and indeed they found it, for in Spain, as well as Spaniards fighting Spaniards, Germans were found fighting Germans, Italians against Italians, and even White Russians against Soviet Russians. The most famous example of this was the battle of Guadalajara in 1937, when the Italian communists in the International Brigade found themselves fighting Mussolini's fascist 'volunteers' for Franco. But in the very battle on the Corunna highroad, of which Boadilla was the culmination so far as Romilly was concerned, Romilly's own German communist commander, who went under the name of Walter (probably a pseudonym, though it has not been possible to discover this for certain) found the body of a German nazi pilot for Franco of the same name.

By the time that Romilly had got to Spain, however, the passage of volunteers for Spain was being organized, and by the international communist movement. After a great deal of vacillation between July and October 1936, Stalin had finally agreed to assist the Spanish Republic with arms and also gave his approval to the organization of assistance to the Republic in the form of volunteers by the Comintern and the Communist Parties of each country. A Comintern delegation visited the Spanish Republican Government and offered to undertake this supply of volunteers, providing the management was under their control. As well as being of military assistance, the international volunteers would do much to publicize the Republican cause. The Republican Government agreed – though they needed arms much more than they needed men – and the establishment of the base at Albacete under André Marty was the consequence. Not all the volunteers for Spain were communists – indeed, Romilly was never formally a member of the Communist Party – but all the important commands of the International Brigade were under communist direction. These international commanders worked quite closely, it would seem, with the Russian military advisers who began to arrive in Spain about the same time. (There were, however, a large group of foreigners who volunteered to fight for the Spanish Republic who did not join the International Brigades but took part where they could, sometimes because they were opposed to the communists. The most famous of these was Orwell.)

The political background to the events described in *Boadilla* is now well-known. The war had begun in July with the Republic directed by a government of men whom it is convenient loosely to speak of as 'liberals'. Under the stress of war and revolution, that government had given way in September to a socialist coalition, in which the prime minister was the veteran socialist Largo Caballero, and in which ministries were allotted to communists as well as socialists and others. In November, just before the battle for Madrid began, this ministry was strengthened by the adhesion of four anarchist ministers, with varying degrees of reluctance at having to exercise power. By November, Franco and the rebel generals had captured about half the land area of Spain, with, however, most of the meat and wheat areas, with less than a third of the population. The greatest cities – Madrid, Barcelona, Valencia, Bilbao – were in government hands, the rebels being established in Saragossa, Seville, Burgos and Salamanca – the latter at this time being General Franco's headquarters. Franco by this time had established himself already as the unquestioned leader of the rebels, being since October head of state as well as head of government, somewhat to the surprise of his Falangist, Carlist and monarchist allies. Both Catalonia and the Basque provinces were virtually independent states within the Republican camp, but the Basque republic was by now cut off from the rest of Republican Spain by the large rebel territories of north Castile. Internationally, the French and the British were still pinning their hopes on non-intervention, and indeed the French had closed their frontier with Spain. But Germany, Italy and Portugal were actively engaged in the war, as was, after October, Russia. Speaking generally, appeasement had not yet entered its gloomiest stage, but Hitler had already (in the preceding February) remilitarized the Rhineland with impunity and Mussolini's rape of Abyssinia had been condoned by the end of sanctions.

Boadilla is one of the few books of the 1930s to retain its freshness and indeed its vigour. The vivid description of battle stands up extremely well. For a book written at nineteen, by someone who had run away from school at fifteen, it is, as it is usual to say (with a pomposity which Romilly himself would have mocked), remarkably mature. At all events it is difficult not to think that in Romilly's death at twenty-three there disappeared not simply a brilliant jester and self-imposed outlaw but someone who was almost certain to have written some most remarkable books. If he had been alive now in 1970, he would be just fifty-two.

Hugh Thomas

Foreword

This book is a personal record of the English Group of the Thaelmann Battalion of the International Brigade in Spain.* This battalion was part of the First International Brigade which took part in the defence of Madrid in October 1936, and was later incorporated in the 11th Mobile Brigade of the Spanish Republican Army. In January 1937, the first complete British battalion was formed at Albacete. For the three months previous to this date, there were two little groups of English people – eighteen members of the Thaelmann Battalion, and another twelve who formed a machine-gun section in a French battalion. This book is about the former of these groups.

This is not a political book, and it is not intended as propaganda. Other people – abler than myself – have presented to the public the true facts of the Spanish situation. Nor is any attempt made to give a history of three months of the Spanish war. This book is the story of the eighteen men who were my companions in the Thaelmann Battalion. No attempt is made to romanticize any of them. I have tried to give a true picture of our life and to show our various relations with one another.

I hope I shall give a picture of people who were by no means fearless fanatics – but very ordinary people drawn from every section of society. Though most of them belonged to the Communist Party, only three could be described as

* Ernst Thaelmann was a German communist leader, arrested after Hitler's coming to power in 1933 and confined to a concentration camp where he died in 1944.

orthodox Marxists. If there was one who deserves the appellation of hero, it must have been Arnold Jeans – a man whose death passed quite unnoticed in England; a Latvian or Russian by birth (no one was ever quite certain which), it was he who held our whole group together and was its leader in the difficult work of rearguard organization as well as at the front. Organization was rendered the more difficult by the variety of our types – Lorrimer Birch, a brilliant scientist and Oxford graduate, sincere and wholehearted communist; Joe Gough, unemployed Luton humorist; Tich, an ex-sergeant of the Buffs, with a kind heart and first-class ability as a quartermaster – that is only to mention three.

To romanticize the Spanish war would be worthless and wrong. To hide men's fears and failings would be, I think, the worst kind of insult. I hope I have done neither. However just a war may be, it must inevitably be a dirty and horrible thing. And when there is inefficiency and mismanagement over-enthusiasm inevitably turns to cynicism. Not that this is a bad thing. For while one realizes how hopeless, how futile, how inefficient something is, one may still realize it is worth fighting for.

At Boadilla del Monte there are no graves nor tombstones. There were no burial speeches, no flags, processions nor trumpets. The bodies of the Englishmen who died there on that December morning lay unburied at the mercy of the Moors. But just as Madrid became a symbol throughout the world of the defence of democracy, so the men who died at Boadilla represent the desire of nearly every Englishman that liberty and justice should prevail.

Chapter I

We walked to the end of the long pier, and he pointed out the once notorious island prison; he knew a lot about everything and talked a lot, but his voice and accent were irritating, and I wished he would speak in French.* He gave a label to each one of the ships we passed. When I was at school there were lots of books about ships and sea adventures and I knew it was supposed to be the thing for boys to want to spend hours pottering about harbours talking to 'old salts'. I have always been hostile to that, among other practical subjects.

Now I began to see the romantic possibilities of ships and harbours. He pointed out French cargo-boats and liners, little sailing-ships from Italy, a Norwegian coal-boat, the swastika emblem flying from a mast away in No. 6 Dock, the black and red flags of the Anarchists flying side by side with the red, yellow and purple of the Spanish Republic. Tomorrow would be Monday; tomorrow, he said, we would go on board some of the ships, we would talk to the captains, perhaps find someone who would do something for me; but best of all, of course, would be to go to the docks. I knew that – I had tramped around them on and off for the last three days, and I had read the 'arrivals' list of the shipping in the newspaper; 'S.S. *Helsingfors*, 4,000 tons, Liverpool, coal and three passengers, going to Rotterdam'; that had been my only draw so far. (Twenty-seven shillings a month normally, but this would have to be gratis, as the captain had no

* The events described in the following paragraphs occurred in September 1936.

authority for signing on extra crew, etc., and cabin boys are not considered necessary by owners, etc., and there were considerations of extra consumption of food for which no allowance, etc.) But anyway, who wants to go to Rotterdam?

We passed a rough-looking sailors' bar. He fumbled in his pocket and then hurriedly pressed a two-franc piece in my hand: 'Here, buy you sandwich, yes?' as he propelled me towards the bar, stepped away himself, seeming to want to show he was in a different class from its patrons. We talked some more. 'You want stay here, Marseille; much good jobs; you speak English, French, German, yes? I fix you well.' I told him that morning's offer. I had been standing watching the passers-by near the Banque de France and a young man (say twenty-seven) came up and asked if I wanted two francs; I said yes, and he gave me a brown paper bag, pointed out a near-by green-grocer's shop, said I must deliver the parcel there and tell the man behind the counter to go to the devil. This I did, giving the message quietly and politely but swiftly, and when he had given me the money he said was I wanting some work, if so to meet him at the same place at three o'clock.

It was already getting dark; I guessed it must be about five o'clock, so I had missed the date; but then it was only half an hour afterwards that I had met my present companion. I was gazing into a pâtisserie at the end of the rue de la République, where it runs into the Place de la Joliette. How hungry the shop window of a pâtisserie makes you feel – I almost decided to spend fourteen sous. He said it was a pretty sight, wasn't it? I looked round to see who it was, then said yes and I could willingly eat the whole window-full. Like an old English gentleman who makes a great show of gallantry in picking up a lady's handkerchief, he went into the shop, and came out with a bag of coconut macaroons.

My story sent him off into a torrent of words and chuckling; 'What sort zis man be, you know? No, p'raps he want zee boy, yes. Zey have much of zees type in zees town; and zey have men who get zee boy for zee rich one, or maybe it for zee Arabs.' Here followed a long description of the various tastes and attractions of Marseilles, with any amount of innuendo and personal inquiry thrown in. I began to think I had been unwise to come with him, instead of keeping the appointment; from his jests and chuckles, I could see he found it amusing that I pretended not to understand some of his remarks, but I think he meant well and understood all right that I hadn't any wish to be sold to the Arabs. His offers of employment boiled down to the suggestion that I should meet crews as they arrived in the harbour and get them to spend their money at someone's cabaret-cum-brothel. 'Yes, zey pay you well, you haz nothing to give for food and sleep, and you get, how you say, one franc for zee ten zey spend.'

Just then we noticed the luxury liner *Mar Caspio*, bound for Valencia with 600 volunteers for the Spanish People's Army.

✳

I didn't like Marseilles but I hadn't done too badly there. I lived five days – and five nights (for these I had to thank the Catholic Charity Organization whose light shines in the rue de la Joliette, where you can stay a week before you have to pay), and my possessions on arrival were: two francs, an English florin, a not very good bicycle, a haversack which contained five shirts and other odd things like a towel and a sweater and a razor and a toothbrush, and *Eyeless in Gaza* and *South Wind*, and a novel by Sinclair Lewis about a rich girl in a rich car who was chased over half North America by a poor man in a poor car. (This was in a paper edition. A month later I used it as lavatory paper.) When I left, I had all these possessions and five francs extra as well.

The first night I didn't know about the light in the rue de la Joliette, and a man showed me to a little café in the Place d'Aix, where the price of the room was one franc fifty; before I saw the old daughter of the old woman who owned the place I never really knew what people meant when they used the word 'slattern'. There was a vile stink which came up from the wash-basin in the 'bedroom'. It was a horrible place, but I had *Eyeless in Gaza* to read. I cursed the carelessness which had brought me there. For only carelessness could have stopped me noticing that if I placed my jacket at a certain angle over the handlebars of my bicycle it was probable that what had been protruding from the breast pocket would no longer be there after a certain number of miles had been accomplished. Thus it came about that some fortunate citizen passing along the road from Valence to Orange was richer by 600 francs, a pound note, a wallet, various letters, a membership card of the Labour Party, and a British passport. This was depressing, as Spain was a long way away; so far that I decided I would do better to bicycle as fast as I could to Marseilles, which was 190 kilometres. Having been born within the sound of Bow Bells, I have always had faith in big cities. But it was still depressing, as, though I didn't for a moment doubt that I should achieve my objective, this wasn't how I had planned to do it. I had pictured myself staying a few days at some place like Perpignan, eating and living comfortably, before embarking on a military diet and existence.

My journey so far from Dieppe (where I had bought a bicycle for 100 francs) had been pleasant and uneventful; I pedalled fast enough during the day to ensure sleeping well after a hearty meal at the little places where I stayed on the road. My main memory of the journey is of the excessive cold of cycling at night. Between Chartres and Orléans at about eight o'clock in the evening I debated with myself the whole question of physical discomfort and 'toughness', decided I must have misunderstood myself when I got bored with a fire and an office and a typewriter, then stopped and drank two cups of hot black coffee with four small glasses of cognac, and changed my mind, and felt marvellously drunk and warm and ready to go on for ever.

✳

In Marseilles I was still on my way to Spain.

It was like this. I have always found selling fairly easy, as I am naturally inclined towards exaggeration and have often been criticized for an over-willingness to talk, and to go on talking. Having been educated up to the school certificate stage at a famous public school (Wellington College), having left rather rapidly and suddenly, and decided it was preferable to support myself on my own labour, having no specialized knowledge of any kind, and not being troubled with an over-quantity of honesty or scrupulousness, it was, I suppose, inevitable that I should soon be selling somebody something. I belong to that very large class of unskilled labourers with a public-school accent.

The first things I sold were my own efforts, and my own productions. But that is fun; that isn't what I consider 'selling'; neither was the sale of my services as a furniture shifter. Silk stockings were the real thing though, for there you can lay your hands on the racketeers – and their victims, the unskilled labourers and, of course, the buyers (though it's no good ever having any sympathy with the buyer!). If anything were to make me anti-Semitic, it would be the silk-stocking racket, for my firm, like nearly every other, was run by Jews. They had a special man whose job it was to 'sell' us on the idea, so that men who had come in with the reservation that if this was a house-to-house canvassing job on a commission basis they weren't having anything to do with it, went away with visions of £10 a week and turned up at 8-45 sharp the next morning.

Having bought a hat, I wasn't altogether a failure at this; with my little black bag of samples under my coat, I rang the bell of prosperous-looking houses on the road into Kent. 'Good morning, would you tell your mistress that Mr. Romilly has called? Ah, good morning, Mrs. Burblebotham, I've called in connection with some propaganda work for the British Textiles Industry; now I don't know whether you were at our exhibition at Manchester House; we found a good many people couldn't get up. I think it was Captain Mackenzie who mentioned your name as being interested in this type of work, so as I was motoring past this way, I thought I'd look you up on the chance.'

(By this time you should be in the drawing-room.)

'Now the matter I'm actually here about has to do with hosiery; please don't run away with the idea I'm going to try and sell you any silk stockings or anything of that kind. But what we are doing, for propaganda purposes, is to demonstrate this guaranteed ladder-resisting all-British silkworm-silk stocking manufactured by British labour to show where this industry stands today in relation to foreign competition.'

Followed the demonstration. I cannot remember every detail, but I know the stocking had a ravel stop, a seamless sole, a double elastic-knit top, a guaranteed unsplittable seam, and that the demonstration ended with a vigorous tug-of-war with your prospective client. After this it was necessary to find out her favourite shades, her size, whether she favoured a long, short or medium 'leg', and then to close: 'Now madam, as I said, I am not attempting to sell you any silk stockings; I haven't any with me if you wanted to buy them. But you have seen for yourself the quality of this hosiery, you have seen our delightful range of shades for all occasions; I don't know when you would next be thinking of ordering some more stockings, shall we say a month from today? And what I suggest is that I should then send you down a dozen trial pairs, made up in your favourite shades, so that you could try them against your present brand.... Shall we say six of musquash, six of flesh? Very well, madam, if you'll just sign here, then I'll give you a receipt for the deposit. As you see, the representative is authorized to collect one shilling per pair only as deposit. Yes, I have change here. Thank you, good day....'

'One shilling per pair deposit only'; and that one shilling, obtained in drawing-rooms all over Kent at the sweat of his brow is the sum total of what this unskilled labourer got out of it.

✳

Mr. John Girton was a Methodist and a teetotaller. He was a small publisher, always ready to give young men a start in his organization. People worked for him for anything from six to eighteen months; a lot of the time they worked for nothing – those were the new ones, of course. When I met him, I was – like everyone – very much impressed; I believed I would soon be making £500 a year, then £1,000 a year; the fact that for the present I was to work, on commission only, for his profit, made no impression on my mind. 'A good man can sell a bad proposition, but a bad man can't sell a good proposition' was Mr. Girton's motto. He was a skilled workman, though, in that he knew all there was to know about publishing, about selling journalism, about printing and printers, blocks and block-makers, paper and paper merchants; but he made his money by selling himself. He sold an idea to men with capital but without brains that he, with his brains, his knowledge and his organization, might increase their capital.

To any enthusiast with from one to ten thousand pounds capital who thought it would be a nice idea to publish a paper on their particular hobby with their particular views, Mr. John Girton came as a godsend. He represented Business and Business Methods, he would get the best prices, he knew the best men to get advertisements, he knew how to deal with the newsagents. And Mr. Girton's staff of young men looking eagerly forward to that time, a few months ahead, when Mr. Girton 'saw no reason why' they should not be earning a considerable income, sweated all day, and sometimes all night as well.

I ran round London interviewing garage proprietors, restaurant and cinema managers, hairdressers, beauty parlours, flower shops, estate agents, private detective agencies, inducing them to advertise in a little diary of London events which we were then occupied with. No one could have been more pleased than myself when I persuaded some garage owner to sign a contract for twenty-six two-inch double column strips at 10s., for which I received £3 in commission. Mr.

John Girton had a grand scheme for dividing up London into districts, and publishing, in this diary, a list of all useful suppliers (garage, car-hiring, sports, fruiterers, etc.) in each district at a small charge for each. 'We'll work the scheme till we can see an aggregate of £60 a week coming in from it, then we'll have to decide whether to put on four more pages for maps and things. Anyway, we'll raise your commission to twenty per cent, so that's £15 a week for you for a start.' That scheme lasted two weeks. Then another took its place.

From silk stockings I had graduated to small publishing. Soon I knew the jargon of space-buyers and 'contras' and bogus circulation figures and rows with printers and sub-Federation rate block-makers. The kind of 'selling' where you ring up people's secretaries to know when you may call, and give someone lunch when they've advertised in your paper is more fun than ringing doorbells in Kent.

When I went to Spain, I had had a job such as this for nine months – the longest time I had ever had the same one for – and was earning £5 a week, which seemed a lot of money. I am mentioning the circumstances of how this job ended, to show how I ever came to fight in a war. If this were a political book, I would explain what I think about the Spanish struggle, which would be reason enough for my wanting to take part in it. The reasons would be much the same as those of the other English members of the Thaelmann Battalion. But I do not think anybody ever does anything just for one clear-cut, logical (in this case political) motive. However strongly I sympathized with the cause of the Spanish people, no doubt if my circumstances in London had been completely satisfactory, I should have gone no further than sympathy. I am assuming it will be taken for granted that everybody who joined the International Brigade had 'political convictions'; but these were not necessarily the only reasons why they joined.

My nine months job was for a film paper whose object was – and, no doubt, still is – 'to give a critical survey of all that is best in films and broadcasting'. Its owners were the people who make documentary films advertising the work of a Government Department.

The head of the unit was well known in Wardour Street and in Bloomsbury. I will call him MacIntosh. In the small circle of his employees and admirers he had assumed an almost superhuman position. Like Sir Oswald Mosley he was known as 'The Leader' or 'The Chief' (the only other person I have come across referred to in this way was the former headmaster and founder of Bedales Coeducational School, and there was a great deal in common between the two men). I believe there are numbers of young men who long to work all day, carrying heavy cameras or opening doors, so that they may have a chance to learn the methods of the Chief.

All this I learned in the course of my first week; I learned it from the reverential way in which his name was mentioned; from the way in which faces lit up at a word of commendation from the great man or clouded with dismay at a rebuke. Mr. MacIntosh had definite opinions about everything, and was at no loss to express them; these opinions were faithfully taken up by his disciples. Like another great man, he was often inclined to deliver a parable. A usual scene would present the Leader at the head of a table with some of the faithful; all would be silent, waiting for the Leader to speak. He would pick on a paragraph in the evening paper, read it out aloud, deliver a pungent comment, and then general conversation could begin.

The Leader was not only brilliant, he prided himself on being tough; that is to say, he would be ready to engage in talk with anyone over a pint of beer in 'public bars as well as the saloons'. When their work would take his unit – say, to film the life of a little fishing village – he was the one to get together with the local characters. Like all great men, like all dictators, the Leader had his critics. There were those unkind enough to suggest that he used sometimes to run fast up three flights of stairs to give his face the right expression of bustle and important work on hand.

For the launching of the paper, there was an editor, a

secretary, an assistant editor, myself (to get some advertise-ments). We worked sometimes fourteen hours a day – as only disciples can work. Then it fell to me to bring two great men together – the Leader, and my former employer, Mr. John Girton. Who better than Mr. Girton could turn the paper into a financial success?

So for a few months I saw the workings of two supermen. When they met, it was the Leader who seemed to become less super. It was the Leader who would listen, fascinated, while the Business Man expounded some gigantic scheme for sending a copy of the *Film Review* to every clergyman in the United Kingdom.

The paper and my work were fun at first. It has always been a good paper, with many first-class contributors, and I looked forward to the steady rise of its advertisement income. On the one hand I had the Leader's vision of a production respected and admired by the *élite* of the film world and all who followed the *élite,* and on the other the Business Man's vision of a giant publishing company with sales and revenue soaring and myself sitting behind a desk with pretty secretaries to do all the work. But it didn't turn out like this.

It is interesting to realize that on an average, two new papers are launched every week, and that only one in twenty survives more than a year at most. If a paper is to be bought and read by members of the public, if it is not some technical production dealing, say, with the insides of motor-cars or retail boot polish sales, then a sufficient number of people must buy it for it to be worth while for advertisers to use the paper as a medium for drawing those readers' attention to his goods.

Mr. Girton drew graphs. The graphs showed two curves rising – advertisements and sales revenue – and one curve falling till it met the other two. The single curve was the costs. The point where the curves met was a few months ahead. The graphs were pinned up in the Leader's office; they were much admired by the Leader and the disciples.

At last the day came, but all the curves had gone in the wrong directions. However, the graph was forgotten. The Business Man now spoke of a vast new 'spending campaign', of leaflets and brochures to be published, of newsagents all over England to be given posters, of publicity with advertisers. It was to be a New Start – the first of many. The Business Man convinced the Leader, the Leader convinced his disciples.

Only one of them had cause for uneasiness. He was the one whose generosity had enabled the paper to be founded, but he seemed glad to be able to do this service for the Leader. The Leader himself was satisfied. Wardour Street was talking about his paper; Wardour Street was talking about him.

My worst moment came when I realized a few of the economic facts of publishing. I reached the conclusion that the *Film Review* would always cost somebody a few thousands a year if we went on trying to launch it in a big way. I knew who would pay all right, and I liked him. So I wrote a long report to try and prove that the paper had no chance of success.

The reply from all the disciples was unanimous: 'Nothing the Chief has ever put his hand to has ever failed!' Illusions of supermen were vanishing fast. I resigned.

The last period had not been over-satisfying. The staff was now vastly augmented. For the editorial side, there was an editor, an assistant editor, a cartoonist, a secretary, and any number of permanent retainers whose names figured on the weekly salary list. Then, too, there was the business staff; Mr. Girton (very much behind the scenes of course as this was but one of his many projects), the accountant, myself, the circulation manager, a few odd business-brightening hangers-on, and the office boy. I had become an assistant manager, so much was there to manage with all the schemes we were working on. As the weather grew hotter in August and the schemes went slower and the costs went higher, a certain demoralization set in; the editors were happily immune, they continued signing on the services of ten-guinea experts. At our end, the circulation manager sweated away addressing the envelopes to the 'free list' all over Europe. I pounded away on a typewriter that I had pleasure in drawing attention to the value of the *Film Review* as a first-class advertisement medium. The office boy brought the papers and tea at five o'clock. At six, we would adjourn and discuss at the nearest pub the story of the two supermen.

Before my notice expired, I had made several rather half-hearted attempts to get another job. Then I had the idea of starting a night-club. With one collaborator, I actually got as far as paying a five pound deposit and taking a lease of two basement rooms in Hart Street; special invitation cards were printed for the opening ceremony. We would have surrealist drawings on the wall; a girl who kept a café would sell me chairs and tables very cheap; some of the negro cabaret performers would help. I wrote to everyone I could think of and got a few promises of cash. It must have been the lingering influence of the Great Business Man which made me so optimistic. Unfortunately, I discovered that, however much could be achieved by optimism, bluff and credit, a solid capital of £100 at least was vital. I had no capital. I had my last week's salary, £5. It was not enough. A pity, as I had the whole thing planned, from evasion of the law to the arrangement of the tables and position of the band.

During my summer holiday I had considered going to Spain. My main objection was still the same – fear that I should be no use, that if any volunteers were needed they would be those who had military experience. I did not even know how to load a rifle. At Wellington College, I had been a pacifist, and had refused to join the O.T.C., so I lacked even that experience. Now that I definitely decided on going, I determined to tell no one of my plan, for fear I should be ignominiously sent back. I told everybody I was going to work on a farm in Belgium.

My job ended on a Friday. On Wednesday I had a party at my flat and auctioned most of the furniture. Altogether I had £9 by the time I left, having paid what I could not help paying. On Saturday morning a registered letter came by post. I opened it eagerly. It was a formal 'Notice to Quit' from my landlord's solicitors. I caught the boat-train for Dieppe that night. Ten days later I was in Marseilles; in three weeks, at the front.

Chapter 2

Outside the ship's dining-room was a notice in French: 'Guard Duties: 7–9 French, 9–11 Germans, 11–13 Italians, 13–15 Yugoslavians, 15–17 Belgians, 17–19 Poles, 19–21 Flemish, 21–23 Russians, 23–1 French, 1–3 Germans, 3–5 Poles, 5–7 Belgians.'

Two men at a time would walk all round the decks, keeping watch and seeing that people did not cluster together. I got on board at five o'clock that afternoon with an Italian and two Polish youths; they were my companions all through the journey. The next morning – and all through that day – the little rowing-boat went backwards and forwards bringing passengers. They arrived in taxis, carrying a haversack or a single suitcase. A few idlers watched apathetically as they left the shore – they looked like week-end excursionists.

It was lucky I had a few books – we waited two days before we moved. The only break in the day was meals – breakfast at half-past six, lunch at half-past ten, supper at half-past five in the afternoon. The various groups kept in their respective nationalities. I was all the time anxious to be efficient and set about getting myself attached to some group, so I was established with the Poles and the Italians. I shared a bed with one of the Poles. He had the frank open face of a boy of fifteen, but he was twenty-eight and had worked in French coalfields for seven years. He showed me a Polish passport and told me he was now a French citizen as he had done his two years' military service.

'Is it very hard?' I asked (we talked in French together).

'It's terrible – but it's useful.'

'Have they all done military service here, do you think?'
I asked. Just then I was very conscious of my shortcomings.
At the office in Marseilles they had asked me what military
service I had done. I told them I had been in my school
O.T.C. That wasn't true, I had refused to join it at
Wellington College, but I was afraid they might not take me
if I admitted this. I had not yet learned to put a true valuation
on the numerous forms we filled in in Spain, or to make a
guess at what became of them, and I was nervous of being
found out. I determined to be a conscientious learner. This
was the only time I ever remember regretting not having
joined the corps. (I need not have done so, of course – it
makes no difference at all whether men are trained or untrained, what matters is that the rank and file should volunteer,
and that their *officers* should have military experience.)

The Pole was my chief friend on the journey. Then there
were two German boys from Toulouse – one was twenty and
the other twenty-three; two of their brothers had been
murdered by the Nazis; we nodded each time we met on deck.
I was surprised to see how many Germans there were. After
the French, they were one of the largest contingents. There
was a Belgian who told me he had deserted from his military
service. The Frenchman in charge of all of us was a very
capable young man. He was twenty-five, tall and fair, and a
member, he told me, of the Central Executive of the Communist Youth International. He was very nice to me and told
me he had not expected to see any Englishmen on the ship.
He asked if I was a student, and seemed a little disappointed
when I told him I wasn't. When I said I was a member of
the Labour Party, he was delighted and treated me with extra
consideration to emphasize the Front Populaire spirit. He
even said he expected there might be a few liberals when we
got to Spain. I was soon drawn into argument with a number
of the French communists – they asked how the Labour
Party's socialist principles were compatible with their accept-
ance of 'non-intervention'. That, of course, I could not tell
them.

There were some very tough guys there – ex-foreign-legionaries, men whose politics had led them to prison. Nearly all of them – as far as I could see – were working-class people.

As we left Marseilles, there was no dramatic exit, no fare-well cheers and saluting. When the ship weighed anchor, a scramble was going on to get into the dining-room for supper. 'Comrades,' said the young Frenchman, 'I beg you, we must have discipline. Let us behave like revolutionaries. Each group must elect a leader who is responsible for everyone. Tomorrow we will issue tickets for the food. Do not scramble for the best places to sleep, there are men here who are ill and they should have the first choice.' It was quite a good dinner – better than any I had had in Marseilles. While we ate, the hungry crowd queueing outside exhorted us to hurry up and finish so that they could have a turn. I had a narrow bed to share with the young Polish miner – we slept with our heads at different ends of the bed.

Outside the harbour of Marseilles, the *Mar Caspio* dropped anchor again, and we did not start off till four in the morning. The sea was rough and that day was not a particularly pleasant one. That evening an order was given for all lights to be extinguished. I was excited. It gave a meaning to the word war. The rest was just a holiday. We saw the twinkling lights of the villages on the Catalonian coast – the *Mar Caspio* was hugging the shore. At ten o'clock we saw Barcelona – a blaze of light like the Blackpool fun-fair. Next morning, we got up at five o'clock, and stood on deck. It was a glorious day and the countryside of Catalonia showed to advantage. '*Quel pays!*' said the fat little chemist from Toulouse, 'but ruined by the bourgeois!'

At ten o'clock we steamed past three French and British destroyers anchored off Valencia. Everyone shouted greetings and sang the Internationale. Some of the sailors on the French ships waved their hands; on the British destroyer an officer looked at us through a telescope. There was no one on the quayside at first. Then we saw little black dots like a swarm of flies in the distance; the swarm grew larger. In twos and threes more figures poured in to fill the gaps until we could make out the enormous crowd that had come to greet us. The cheers and salutations went on for an hour. The young Frenchman made another speech:

'Comrades, please show perfect order. Let me ask those of you who are communists, and particularly the French communists, to set an exanple. Be last with getting the food; first with helping someone else. Keep in your groups. Show our Spanish comrades that we have discipline as well as enthusiasm.'

I was a bit uneasy. My Polish friend had disappeared, and now they were calling out the different nationalities. I tacked myself on to the French chemist – he was part of the Toulouse Communist French group. At last it was our turn to disembark. It was very hot. A lorry was waiting into which we threw coats and haversacks. The procession stretched out of sight down the road – here and there a few ragged banners with slogans chalked in white – here and there a gap with a man marching by himself trying to get them to march in step. The crowd went with us, jostling along the pavements or walking in our ranks. A lot of vivas, and always the slogan *'No Pas-ar-án,' 'No Pasarán,'* were the words one caught from the crowd's cheering. The Frenchmen, led by a cheer leader, shouted *'Vive le Front Populaire,' 'Vive la République,'* then copied the crowd's *'No Pasarán.'*

That is the only impression I have of Valencia – a huge, cheering crowd, a hot and tiring march down interminable streets, slogans and posters and military flags and badges everywhere. Some of the Frenchmen shouted: *'Les Soviets Partout! Les Soviets Partout!'* others reproved them; no sectarianism.

We reached a barracks, and assembled in its big open square. There were speeches from the balcony above. A band played the Internationale, then the Spanish National Anthem, then the Marseillaise; 'First thing on the agenda, and most important,' said the speaker, 'food.' We cheered heartily.

After lunch there were more speeches – a new figure was introduced whom I took to be the supreme head of everything, André Marty, the famous French revolutionary and Communist Deputy.* He told us a theatre performance had been organized for us that afternoon. 'And after supper this evening, a special train will take you to Albacete, to join the International Column.' This was the first time I had heard that name, the first time I knew that we were part of an organized contingent of foreign volunteers.

After the speeches we hung about in the yard another hour. There were a few old rifles lying about the sheds and I watched carefully men who picked them up and practised aiming. I decided to confess my ignorance, and asked a kind-looking Frenchman to explain the system of the thing to me. He showed me how to hold the rifle butt pressed against my shoulder, and how to shove back and close the bolt. I regarded this as the first stage of my military science – now I knew how to fire a rifle so long as it had nothing in it. There was a gymnasium where men were lifting dumb-bells and climbing ropes and doing strong-man turns. I found I was very much out of condition.

The music-hall show was better than an average high-class London entertainment of its kind, though it had been arranged at the last moment.

Everyone had been moved by our reception, and was anxious to preserve the spirit of goodwill. When a section of the audience started cheering a tenor on his way to a top note, the rest looked round with angry 'Sh-shs.' Then a Spaniard told us they always cheered in the middle of performances like that. A crowd followed us all the way to the theatre and back again.

Before supper we were warned of the strength of the wine.

* André Marty (1886–1956) had first come to public notice in 1919 as the leader of the French naval mutiny at Odessa which sought to avoid French intervention in the Russian civil war. In 1936 he was a member of the Executive Committee of the Comintern (Third International).

It made no difference to the little French chemist – he drank up two full bottles and was then prepared to lead the whole company into action – nothing later than that very night would satisfy him. A very tough and wiry foreign legionary, who was also part of the Toulouse group, took charge of him. The leader was a harassed man of about thirty, who closely resembled a boy I knew at school; he had a podgy face and found his work difficult, especially after the wine. The main problem was to keep everyone together. He arranged places for us all in five ranks of four each, but there was always someone lost in another section.

At ten o'clock we marched to the station and boarded the special train. Our welcome on arrival was surpassed here. The crowd was so enormous that we continually got caught up in it on our way. The train waited a long time in the station before moving off, and free kisses were given to anyone who leaned his head out. We learned new slogans: *'Viva las señoritas españolas'* and *'Viva Vino Blanco.'* In the first hour the train stopped at every little station on the way – and at each one there was the same crowd, the same friendly words, the same forest of clenched fists as we moved on. That was the agreeable part.

The rest of the journey – when the cheering and shouting was over – was not so good. It was an eight hours' ride, with wooden seats and every compartment crammed out. The after-effects of a first-class supper were a sweating garlicky mass of men, sprawling on the floor under seats and sleeping on the racks – we would take it in turns for the seats. I had continual attacks of diarrhoea all through the night. It was cold and bleak and wintry when we reached our destination. In the scuffle of forming up in the station, I lost my group, and was attached to the Russians. We went to a barracks and flung ourselves down on mattresses to sleep. My diarrhoea went on till midday. At supper that night I learned where we were – Albacete, midway between Madrid and the coast.

✳

I was four days with the Russians at Albacete. They were curious, kind and interesting people. There were fourteen of them, and they all came from Paris. They belonged to an association of Russian *émigrés*, formerly Whites, now anxious to return to their homeland. A. (I call him A. because I could never spell or pronounce his name) spoke English perfectly. He had been attached to a transport division of Kolchak's White Army during the Russian revolution, and later got a job with an American company in Paris as a chauffeur and mechanic. 'We had the choice, six years ago,' he told me, 'of regaining Russian citizenship. I didn't take it. There are a lot of Russians in Paris who would have seen I didn't get a job if I had done so. I hadn't the sense then to realize what it meant. This is a good opportunity.' I had noticed A. first in the train from Valencia – he had been talking English with an Italian who had lived many years in America; we called this man the Italian gangster.

The leader of the Russian group was called Sokolinoff. I was told he had been a Cossack leader, and he looked like a character from *Anna Karenina*. Then there were one or two tall broken-down old men; they were rather mad; you might have taken them for slobbering old women; but the maddest and strangest of them all was Nono. Nono was huge and fat and old. His face had a puzzled childish expression, and he would fly into rages if he thought he was being baited; when this happened you could see his lips curl up then move quickly in violent speech, but unless you were standing close you could make nothing out of his mumble. Nichol was probably the only normal member of that party. Waiting about in barracks the first day, I watched him exhibiting his muscles, and inquired respectfully to know what was the recipe for his strength. He explained he had worked for ten years in a French factory where he had to lift something or other continually and also that he was a professional boxer. He and A. were my chief friends.

Also attached to the group, but very different in character from any of them, was the Little Latvian. He was as talkative

34

and bright as the Russians were silent and sombre – he was
very friendly and often invited me to come along with him
and buy wine or sweets; he munched peanuts, and said he
adored England and English people. 'But you see they say
No. I can't come in. When they got to Southampton I clapped
my hands, I knew I would like England, though I never go
there before; and I thought I could do more – how do you
say – trade with Englishmen. But the police he say no. So
I had to go back to Latvia.'

I was interested in his history at first, but got heartily sick
of it by the time I had heard every incident of it a dozen times.
His lack of complete command of English idiom made his
stories drag on interminably. Sometimes I would get so in-
furiated I would interrupt: 'Yes, well, then what after?' or
'Oh, I see, so you had quite a good business year, very interesting. . . .' He was very kind and very generous, but he
was not an ideal companion and he looked like a guinea-pig.
Nono hated him.

On the second night we were allowed from six till twelve
o'clock out of barracks. The Little Latvian offered me a meal
in the town and I accepted gladly. Wherever we went, Nono
stumbled on ten yards behind. 'He is craazee,' said the Little
Latvian, 'I don't know what we should do about heem, he
follow us.' Eventually Nono joined up with us, and he
bought me a drink. From what he said, it appeared he mis-
trusted the Latvian, and was anxious for my welfare. He had
nothing to drink, but all the time gave you the impression of
a drunkard; he roared with laughter and explained he could
see the Little Latvian knew no English really – he only
pretended to. It was a queer evening.

Those few days were mostly spent in resting, waiting,
finding out the people in one's section, forming up in the road
and marching from the barracks where we slept to the barracks where we ate, more waiting, then the principal thing of
the day, a plate of soup followed by a plate of hash, and
sometimes a pomegranate at the end.

On the second day we marched to a big stretch of open

ground outside the town. I thought we were going to start drill or manoeuvres; but it was waiting again, and then a Frenchman in uniform made a speech. He said he knew everyone was impatient to start, he knew everyone was impatient with the arrangements; would we all realize they had had to make the start – arranging the feeding, the clothing, the organizing; we ought not to grumble if we had to wait till five o'clock for our lunch. In Albacete there were just over 1,100 of us; here, in this field, were less than 700; yes, he knew that there were some in orderly duties, that there were some on the kitchen staff, that there were men sick; but it was disgraceful. Most of all, he blamed the group leaders, they were responsible for seeing each individual member received the orders. If they were not capable of doing their job, then other leaders must be elected. Now to pass on to the future, he was sure all comrades would see to it that this sort of thing did not occur again. Very soon we would have equipment and rifles, then proper training would start. At the moment, these things were lacking; but did that mean we would continue idling about? It did not, and he knew we would agree that this should not be so. Tomorrow morning, at seven o'clock, we would assemble in this same place for the beginning of some vigorous physical training.

Next morning I was glad to find the physical training did not amount to much. We split up into groups and did any exercises that occurred to us. The Russians played leap-frog most of the time – marching, or doing exercises with them, I was in an almost hysterical state of giggles. They were never in step. Nono invariably took heavy measured paces, and though, for a few minutes, these might coincide with someone else's, his tempo was different and it was inevitable he would soon be out of step. Sokolinoff and Nichol would try to introduce a little smartness, but the heavy influence of the stragglers was always too much for them. During the exercises, they panted and heaved and sweated; they were like pieces of rusty old machinery.

They took the names of everyone who had had no military

experience. I thought it best to confess, though I was dismayed to see there were barely fifty of us from the whole assembly. The Little Latvian was with me. We were called together into one group and made to practise marching, right-turning, and about-turning. There was a long dispute about the various methods of turning right-about – French, English and German. We never agreed which was correct.

The next day I was with the Russians on a 'fatigue' duty. We cleaned up the square and the whole barracks and dining-room. I was glad to have some work to do, and went enthusiastically for the garbage and latrines. I was looking forward to having this work to my credit – I felt at last I was earning something, doing something; in the same way I had been glad of the miserable discomfort of the train journey from Valencia – I thought of it all as a toughening process which I needed. The Russians had been a relief – it really seemed there were other people as inefficient as myself. All the same, they were unreal, that was why I welcomed the latrines. An elderly Frenchman, with a kind face, who was making a tour of inspection with André Marty, said to me: 'Young people, they think war is something romantic, something terrible; they think of bayonets, and charges and courage, but they are wrong. This, this cleaning of plates and sweeping, and counting clothes, this is war.'

Later in the morning we did the kitchen work. The man in charge – he was in charge of the kitchen and the feeding arrangements every day, so he was quite an important person – was a Frenchman, about thirty-five. He had two main characteristics – one was always to look preoccupied, worried and importantly angry; the other was the ability, at all times, to carry less than half an inch of cigarette stub in his mouth. I gave him the wholesome respect he seemed to require, but I must admit he was not an agreeable man. By the end of that day I was exhausted.

At nine o'clock we were serving the second dinner – if you were holding the soup, your arm ached by the time you got to the end of one table – and there were curses and demands

37

for bigger helpings, but it was a pleasant atmosphere. Then the lights were turned out. A few seconds' silence, then the inevitable humorists started up, and there was the same chatter as before. At the door, a man shouted:

'Silence, air-raid!'

This time there was absolute quiet for a minute at least, then gradually, in whispers, the chatter began again; the whispering would rise and fall, most of the noise coming from men saying: 'Sh – sh – discipline, comrades, discipline.' Just then I did not think of the wickedness and frightfulness and horror of air bombardments – I was wildly excited. This was the nearest thing to war I had seen since they turned out the ship's lights off the coast of Catalonia. In the darkness outside all faces were turned upwards – we could see nothing, hear nothing.

A. was very drunk. He was in the centre of the front row of our group as we marched back to the barracks – we swayed first to one pavement, then to the other. The Russians were carrying bottles of strong Spanish wine – one was uncorked, passed round to each man, then spilled into the road. It was an exciting evening. Self-appointed guardians of the peace saw that no one smoked. 'Put out that match this instant,' and a sentry would rush up with fixed bayonet, threatening a Russian who was lighting a cigar. We were playing at soldiers.

Chapter 3

Westmount, Province of Quebec, Canada, started as a suburb of Montreal. It expanded rapidly at the beginning of this century, acquired its own town hall, electric plant and water works, and became an independent city. The register of births in the city of Westmount dates from 1911. William James Gough – born January 28th, 1911 – is the first name on Westmount's register.

At Walter Street Council School in Luton, Bedfordshire, where William James Gough's parents settled soon after his birth, he called himself Number One Citizen of Canada. His parents called him Jamie. I thought his name was Joe. Joe started as a butcher – at the age of twenty-one his hands, his expression and his permanently red face suggested this trade. But when he finished his apprenticeship he was unable to get a job in this trade, and became a metal finisher in the Vauxhall Motor Works.

Joe's political and social life was more important than his work. The debating club of the Vauxhall works and the music society were his main centres of activity – and his weapons, in the first case, communism, in the second, the double bass. The two went together. In 1935 Joe had saved up enough money to go to Russia for a holiday; his communism was stronger when he came back, because he had been so impressed with the open air singing and dancing in the parks of Moscow. Next year Joe went to Germany. He took with him a number of fascist badges and emblems captured in street frays with Luton Blackshirts, and lived practically free for five weeks, hitch-hiking and staying in youth hostels. That was after his employment with the Vauxhall Motor Works had come to a close – but Joe's friends there still made him come and play the double bass one evening every week. He made up his mind very soon after the Spanish war started, and got the money to go to Paris. The person Joe most minded leaving was his mother, but he never doubted that he would return to Luton with a Spanish general's uniform and put the Public Assistance officials in their places.

✳

Harry Addley was so small that his men automatically called him Tich. That was when he was a sergeant in the Buffs in the World War. The name stuck – he was called Tich when he was a group leader in the Thaelmann Battalion in Spain. During four days of the greatest slaughter in history – the battle of the Somme – thousands of Englishmen lay dead and dying in No-Man's-Land. Tich was able to climb into a shell-hole. It was all he could do, for a piece of shrapnel was lodged in his thigh. He was there all the four days. After the War he kept a restaurant in Dover. 'Harry's' was well known, it and its owner were well liked. All Tich's organizing ability went into it. He did the cooking. His partner was his greatest friend, Arthur Ovenden; this man had gone into the War as a pilot at the age of seventeen. Both were communists. They did not have a sudden impulse to go and fight in Spain – they thought it all out carefully before they decided that their experience would make their services some use to the Spanish people. They took their own boots and their own uniform with them. They met Joe in Paris and liked him. Joe was mad, of course, but he was English, and that was a relief from the carriage loads of Frenchmen and Germans and Poles who were with them on the train to Marseilles. There were two other Englishmen there; they kept to themselves all the way, so it was natural Joe should join up with them. Messer, the one with the square chin and ginger beard, was a communist – but they didn't know about Norman.

Norman was Messer's pal; he was a Roman Catholic, he hadn't got the same sort of credentials. Then there were Jerry and Aussie.

✳

Aussie did not like France. He was an Australian tramp, thirty, and looked forty. His name was Whateley; we called him Aussie. In the hot weather of August 1936, he slept on the benches of the boulevards of Montparnasse. He had no friends. He had got a job on a cargo-boat from Mexico to le Havre, as they had told him he would get work there. He could not speak French, though now after six months on roads and benches he could understand what they said. But they had no time for a man who could not talk. Aussie wished he was back in Mexico – back with the generous peasants whose creed forbade them ever to refuse food to the penniless traveller. He knocked on doors in France and they gave him great hunks of bread – greyish bread, brown bread, plenty of it, but always bread. Aussie had been ten years in Mexico – he had all the kindliness of the Spaniard, none of the quick warm intelligence of the Frenchman. There was a war in Spain – it was quite simple to Aussie – the eternal conflict between the peasant and the landowner, the worker and the capitalist. He did not need books for that analysis.

But on that bench of Montparnasse in August, Aussie was as low as he had ever been. He knew it. He knew that in a month or two he would no longer care about getting bread. The spirit which had taken him from Australia to England and across four hundred miles of Indian Mexico did not exist here – the bright sophistication of the café was too much for him. He thought of England. But it would soon be winter. England and English people were no use in the cold weather. That would get him lower even than Paris.

Aussie told a Catholic welfare society that he wanted to go and fight for the people in Spain. And the Catholic society gave him ten francs and a ticket for Marseilles. It was in Marseilles that he met Jerry.

Jerry's name was Fontana. Two of the fingers of his left hand were missing – he had been injured in an explosion in a munitions factory in America. He had a job as a docker in Marseilles. They paid well, but Jerry reckoned it would cost him too much in doctor's fees if he carried on. He was too small for the work. Jerry hadn't any politics, except to look after himself. But when he met Aussie, he thought perhaps there was something in this Spanish idea, so he managed to get on the ship that was taking Aussie and Joe and Tich and Babs and Norman and Messer to Valencia with 2,000 other volunteers. This was four days after I had left – I was already in Albacete. Jerry made a few hundred *pesetas* on the journey over, but he did not talk much. Aussie didn't talk at all.

✳

Lorrimer Birch was communist. His communism was a thing which lasted seven days a week. He had never known hunger, nor oppression, nor fighting. He was a graduate of Cambridge, twenty-four years old, he worked in the office of a research chemist, he was a good scientist, and he lived in Hampstead. There were street meetings, demonstrations, processions and clashes with fascists. Birch was not sure if his work in Hampstead was not too important – but his colleagues gave him permission to go to Spain. His parents lived in Australia. He told his friends that his sister was ill, that he had to go and visit her. It was an elaborate business. He kept a diary of all that time – his diary included the detailed deception; it included the impressions of the girl who was not interested when he went, and the indecision about travelling by a service which only offered first and second class. His diary says he thought a good deal about the writing of a 'Last Will and Testament' before he left. On the journey to France, and through France to the Spanish frontier, he spent all the time learning Spanish. Then he had two days at the little town of Cerbère, before his communism got him past the frontier.

When he reached Barcelona (early in September), Birch was one of the very first members of the English Tom Mann Centuria* – the leader of that centuria was a Stepney man called Nat Cohen. The others were Bill Scott, an Irishman and ex-member of the I.R.A., Raymond Cox, a young Southampton clerk, David Marshall, a boy of twenty-three who had been an assistant on a Public Relief Committee, and brought copies of Keats and Swinburne and Shelley to Barcelona, and Sidney Avenger, called Long Sid on account of his unwieldy bulk, a Jewish student from a London university. Bill was Irish, which made a difference, but the other three came readily under Birch's influence. So, too, did Jock Gillan, a lorry-driver from Gorbals, Glasgow. He liked them all. He put up with Jock's swearing and Sid's clumsiness and Bill's Irishness. And they all respected Birch and looked up to him.

These men were all communists and all, in one degree or another, came under Birch's influence, and recognized Birch's qualities of leadership and organization. Keith Watson and Donovan were the only ones who weren't communists. Don was Irish, and that made an extra difference too. Keith Watson was a bit over-cynical and laughed at Birch.† He was always rushing off to Barcelona and not taking any of the rules and regulations seriously enough.

But Birch was a communist first of all, and it was part of his creed to co-operate sincerely with people he didn't like – he was determined his communism shouldn't interfere with his fairness of judgement. His best friend at Barcelona was Arnold Jeans. Jeans was the group's mystery man; all his front teeth were missing, which gave a humorous twist to his speech; he spoke English with a slightly foreign accent – and

* Tom Mann (1856–1941) was for many years a prominent labour leader who after 1919 became a communist.

† Keith Scott Watson later decided that he would prefer to be a journalist rather than fight. See below, page 112 and his own book, *Single to Spain*, London, 1937, and Sefton Delmer, *Trail Sinister*, London, 1961, page 304.

he spoke five other languages as well. No one knew for certain whether he was a Russian or a Latvian or a Pole. They knew he had been through the Russian revolution as a boy, that he had a revolutionary past, that he had been imprisoned and deported from several countries, that he had six passports in his possession. He did not say much or make himself prominent at that time. But Birch knew he was a good communist all right.

Birch was all for discipline, but even more insistent on democratic control; it was he who inspired the Group Meetings which became almost the main events of their time at Barcelona. These lasted anything from two to five hours, and would start with the chairman reading out an agenda, which might be as follows: – Number 1, Discipline; Number 2, the French comrades; Number 3, Propaganda; Number 4, the Keith Watson affair; Number 5, Political Commissar's Duties: '... Now will anyone make any suggestions as to the order these should be taken in.' Follows a ten-minute debate. Since Keith and Donovan were not party members, Birch favoured the idea of having a communist faction meeting before each Group Meeting to decide what attitude the communists should take at the Group Meeting. Keith made a lot of cracks, but his appreciative audience was small. Birch laughed and Dave Marshall laughed, and that was about all; Don laughed too, because he didn't like communists much; Bill smiled.

Like most of the quiet kind of Irishmen, Bill Scott had a very nice personality, and a way of saying humorous things in an aggrieved kind of manner which made them funnier. He liked Keith and found Keith's urban experience useful in finding out all that Barcelona had to offer in the way of entertainment. Everyone liked Bill. He had been a member of the Irish Republican Army. They elected him political responsible.

The Tom Mann Centuria stayed six weeks in Barcelona. They did a little training as machine-gunners and had a good time. They were impatient to go to the front – and early in

October they applied to leave Barcelona and join the International Column at Albacete. Their leader decided to stay – a few months later he was wounded leading an attack on the Huesca front. Then Lorrimer Birch was elected Group Leader.

Chapter 4

On the wall of the barracks at Albacete was pinned each morning the front page of the *Mundo Obrero*. Next to it was a reproduction of an article in a Russian newspaper, which proclaimed in five-inch headlines that the peril of Leningrad in 1918 was greater than the peril of Madrid today. The Germans had a printed notice entitled 'Discipline'. 'We exalt discipline.' In French was an exhortation not to render ourselves unfit for service by getting diseases at brothels. There was nothing much else to do, so we read all these notices right through every time. But now there were signs of activity. Some men had been given rifles and equipment, and on the third day, 400 formed up in the square – they were heavily laden, and as well as their ordinary equipment, they had any amount of pots and pans and spoons and knives hanging from their belts.

The Little Latvian came to me excitedly next morning: 'You see, I say there were Engleeshmen here'; he pointed out a little group of figures standing in the square, distinct in khaki uniforms. 'You ask them,' he went on, 'if I can come too. I want to be with ze Engleesh.' Birch and Marshall were the first ones I talked to. Marshall said: 'Can you give us any lowdown on this place here?'

I asked if they were all English, how many of them there were. 'We've got two lots, one English, one Scotch,' someone said. 'I can see he's Scotch,' I answered. I meant Jeans – the one who looked as if he was the leader, but I was wrong about his accent. They told me Birch had been elected leader.

'Well, what the devil's going to happen here?' said Birch.

'It looks as if we were going to be kept waiting about like we were in Barcelona.'

'Ay,' said Bill, the Irishman, 'we'd ha' done much better in Barcelona.'

I met Keith at lunch. We had a few friends in common in London. 'Are you one of the faithful?' he asked me.

'Faithful? How do you mean?'

'Member of the Communist Party, I mean, you know, see the holy light.'

I told him I belonged to the Labour Party.

'It's religion, you know,' he went on. 'You'll have enough of it in the next few weeks. Have you joined our lot yet?'

I told him about the Russians.

'D'you think I could join up with that lot, too?' he said at the end. 'Nono sounds heaven.'

After lunch I saw Sokolinoff dashing across the yard, with a rifle over his shoulder. He saw three of the Russians standing together, and gave them some message. I went up to find out what was happening, apparently they all had orders to get equipment and ammunition. Perhaps this meant they were leaving for the front. 'What do we do? Where do we get it?'

'It's not for you,' said Sokolinoff, 'only for those who've been soldiers.'

'Where are you going, then?' I asked. 'Isn't it for guard duty?'

He said, 'Madrid,' but I laughed at the idea of this. I thought they must be going to the training camp. Anyway, I determined not to be left out now something was happening at last (those four days had been very long). The Little Latvian was not very enthusiastic, but I persuaded him to find out exactly what was happening, and later on we both went to the stores to get our equipment and rifles. There was a big queue there; they were all turned away, there was no more equipment.

Afterwards I met Birch and Jeans and Marshall in the street. I was with the Little Latvian; he greeted them effusively. 'Is there any way of telling him in Latvian to — off?' said Birch in an undertone. That evening I shifted my things, and joined the English group, who had three cubicle rooms for sleeping. 'Of course you'll have to be elected, you know,' said Birch, 'before you actually join officially, but there won't be any difficulty about that. We're having a Group Meeting anyway tonight, so we'll pass it through formally then.'

I was dismayed to learn that they had all received training at Barcelona, as machine-gunners. Next day, on the parade ground, everyone's speciality was written down. Someone suggested we should stake our claim as fully trained machine-gunners. I need not have worried. It would not have made any difference what they wrote down.

The Group Meeting – and all the subsequent Group Meetings – were the most important events. With Birch as proposer and Marshall as seconder, I was unanimously elected a member, and received congratulations from all on the honour. The two main points the meeting discussed were discipline and the question of which nationality group we should join. There were ten of us, and it was obvious we could not do anything on our own. They were unanimous when it came to a question of asking to join the French or the Germans; a majority of ten to one favoured the latter, and I was the one. There were strong criticisms of the habits of 'our French comrades' that they had experienced at Barcelona; language was the only argument I could think of, but then Jeans spoke perfect German so he could act as interpreter. Jeans didn't talk much during the meeting. Birch and Keith and Bill and Marshall talked the most – it was not difficult to see the idea of these Group Meetings was due to Birch's inspiration, he was always talking about points of order, and electing chairmen, and proposing resolutions – but when I laughed at it all, he laughed too. We came on to discussing discipline.

There was a long discussion about whether the leader should have power to order punishments, – eventually we agreed to elect a tribunal of three who would decide this question after an accusation of bad conduct had been made by the leader. Keith was one of the members. He said that would be a good thing as he was one of the chief offenders and could be relied on to deal thoroughly with others. (He told me of his latest offence: 'These people are absolutely dictators, you know; on the way in the train I met a very nice girl, so I went and sat with her in her compartment, and everthing was going fine, you know, and then that great silly Sid, can't mind his business ever that great stiff, comes barging in and says: "Oh, you can't sit there, you've got to come in the same compartment with us," so I said — you; and what do you think they did, put me under military arrest – military arrest! All this stuff about "being in a state of war" because they haven't found someone to get off with themselves. . . .')

Keith and Don and I shared a cubicle together. 'Don snores a bit,' said Keith, 'but it's better than being with Jock.' Jock, who overheard the remark, gave him suitable punishment, first with words, then with a pail of water. Jock and Sid were the two rowdy ones of the party, particularly Jock. That night I thought to myself that, on the whole, I was very lucky in my companions. I had expected them all to be tougher, more frighteningly efficient. I tried to sort them all out. People like Birch and Keith and Marshall were fairly easily placed; so was Jock; so was Ray, he was patently nice and helpful, really I put him and Birch and Marshall together; for one thing, they were all about twenty-two. Sid was a bit different. Then there were Bill and Donovan, from Belfast and Dublin; I liked Don, though he seemed a little mad. Bill was efficient – I thought of him as one of the leaders. And, of course, you couldn't put Jeans into any category at all.

Next morning we all in turn visited the Political Commissar. 'This is to test how politically sound you are,' said Keith. The Political Commissar had been appointed to look after all non-military questions, such as clothes, food, leaves out of barracks, complaints, etc., as well as all political questions.

49

The Little Latvian joined us, though Keith and myself were probably the only ones who would have wished him to be a member of the group. I thought he would make it amusing. But when he saw the Commissar he told him he belonged to a party – but the 'party' he mentioned was a town in Latvia. Jeans said afterwards that it turned out he had a very shady record altogether, so on these grounds we got rid of him. But three months later he was still at Albacete, buying macaroons and coffee with milk (when milk was a great luxury), so he did not do so badly.

The Commissar was a German. He asked us our name, age, occupation of our parents, whether they knew we were in Spain, what political party we belonged to, and, last: 'Why have you come to Spain?' This was an easy one, the poster on the barracks wall proclaimed the answer: 'To smash fascism.'

We were on guard duty that day, and for the first time I was given a rifle. Birch showed me how to load it; he explained how to bring the cartridge from the barrel to the breech. I still did not know how to insert a clip of cartridges all at once or how to take the pieces to bits for cleaning. We were supposed to stop anyone going out of the barracks and ask all coming in for their papers. I was with Sid. 'We must really see how many we can catch and send back. Did you hear the commandant congratulating the English on being the best guards?' he said.

We were on guard again that night with the Germans. The Germans had arrived in the afternoon. Birch had known some of them in Barcelona – they had been part of the Thaelmann Centuria which had fought on the Huesca front. They had recaptured Tardienta and had once actually got into the streets of Huesca – they had joined the other Germans who had come by boat and were now almost as numerous as the French. In the guard-room that evening they sang till midnight – magnificent bass and tenor voices. One of their officers told us the latest news. 'Toledo was captured by the Government troops. Russia was about to declare war on

Germany. One thousand rebels had surrendered on the Madrid front.'

But there were other rumours – 'Madrid had fallen.' We did not think much of them. All this time newspaper placards in England proclaimed that the rebels were about to enter Madrid. To us it wasn't so important, so real. Madrid was not then the most famous name in the headlines of the world's newspapers. We realized perfectly that if Madrid fell the war would go on. I never even imagined we would go to Madrid. It was only one front out of many.

When Keith went on guard duty Sid took his mattress. Keith came back when his spell was over, and fumed for a few minutes. Sid muttered: 'Find yourself another place,' so Keith hit him on the leg with the butt of his rifle. Next day there was a Group Meeting about it, and Keith was accused 'of assault with firearms'. Even Ray said: 'Serious thing that, you know.' Keith and Sid were never on good terms.

We had baths that day – my first since England. Birch told me we could go along afterwards to the Café de Albacete as he had heard there were some other Englishmen there. This was quite a joke with us – every day we were being asked had we heard about the forty Englishmen at the training camp or the Irish battalion at Madrid, so I said: 'I expect it's some more Latvians.' But there they were, nine of them drinking coffee, when we arrived. A very different lot from our group, I thought. Older and tougher. A broad, heavy-set man did most of the talking – it was mostly grumbling about the conditions and organization of everything. This was Ovenden – Babs they all called him, didn't realize at first that this group possessed one of the most necessary qualifications for any army – the ability to curse everyone and complain of everything. 'What we've been doing here is waiting about and eating and then waiting about for the next bit of grub. Then they've started some jolly game of hauling ourselves out at six in the morning to go on parade and listen to some fat bastard gassing his head off in some language we don't understand. When someone tried to get us up this morning, we just stayed fixed where we were.'

Most conspicuous of the new lot was a youngish man with a ginger beard whom I remembered having seen in the Fitzroy Tavern.* This was Messer. I liked him and Norman best of the lot. Norman came along to see us that night, and we asked him to give us the lowdown on his crowd: 'Well, let's see,' he said. 'There's Babs and Tich to begin with. Babs came out here as an airman, he had a pilot's certificate from being in the War or something, only I think he's getting a bit sick of being mucked about. Tich and he are the ex-soldiers, you know, always make their own arrangements for everything. Then there's Messer, he's with me.'

'The one with the beard?'

'Yes, that's him. Then there's the little American who came on at Marseilles, Jerry, we call him, and the fellow who came with him, Aussie, he's a bit of a queer bird. There's another fellow, I've forgotten his name, a student I think, rather a la-di-da kind of chap. Then of course there's Joe.'

'Is that the extraordinary-looking fellow with the red face and glasses?' someone asked.

Norman sighed. 'Well, I'll try and give you some lowdown about him. When he came out here he brought a complete blackshirt outfit with him, said he'd stolen it from the fascist headquarters in Luton. And he's bought a brand-new suit, to go home with and march up and down Luton High Street. Can you beat it? He's got an amazing collection of stuff, bangles and rings and things, says they're for the Spanish señoritas; and he goes on collecting more and more gear, knives and bits of string and old bandages.'

Norman told us he himself had been driving lorries around for the last few days. 'I met a friend of yours,' he said. 'The chap I'm working with, a Russian chauffeur. Amazing man. He can't keep off the booze, every time you go out he wants to stop for a drink. I'm prepared to be on the bum as much

* Public house on the corner of Windmill and Charlotte Streets, London. At that time, and in the 1940s, a Bohemian rendezvous.

as anyone, but that fellow is certainly a champion sponger. Still, he's a damned good mechanic; when these lorries arrived he took every one of the engines to pieces, the instructions are all written in Russian, he's about the only chap who can understand them. God knows what they'd do without him.' The brand-new Russian lorries rumbling through the streets with loads of clothes and food and munitions were now a familiar sight in Albacete.

I only saw A. once again. We drank a bottle of wine, and I remember him saying: 'This is all very interesting. Some men want to rush and fight at once. They are silly. There is a great deal to do here.' The other Russians I never saw again.

Next day was my eighth in Albacete. We were told to pack our haversacks and march to another barracks, where the rest of the English were quartered. This time I noticed Joe at once. 'You want a hair-cut,' he said to me. 'I've got a pair of shears upstairs; if you like to nip up and fetch 'em I'll give you a once-over now.'

Birch said to me: 'I don't know whether these people will come into our lot or not, or if they'll accept me as leader.' While he was talking about this I was straining my ears to listen to a story Norman was telling.

André Marty was there, standing with a little group on a balcony above – it was very like the scene at the barracks at Valencia. His speech lasted half an hour, and I took down notes to translate it to the others afterwards. He said: 'The Spanish people, and the Spanish People's Army have not yet conquered Fascism. Why? Is it because they have lacked enthusiasm? A thousand times no. Is it because they have lacked courage? I say ten thousand times no. But they have not won. There are three things that they have lacked, three things that are essential for victory, three things which we must have – which we will have. The first is political unity; the second is military leaders; the third is discipline.'

These themes were enlarged on; he pointed out that those who came to fight this war were no longer communists or socialists or republicans or radicals – they were anti-fascists. When he spoke of military leaders, he introduced the stubby figure on his left, with his record of fighting in the Red Armies of Russia and China: 'General Emilio Kleber.'* A roar of applause greeted Kleber as he stepped forward and gave the clenched fist salute. I lost the sense of the next part of the speech, after he had once more introduced the Political Commissar of the Brigade.

Later on I noted: 'There are those who are impatient, who wish to rush off to the front at once, untrained, without proper arms. I say those people who spread those ideas – though they mean well – they are criminals. We are preparing for war, not for massacre. When the first International Brigade goes into action, they will be properly trained men, with good rifles, a well-equipped corps.' The next bit I missed until the end: 'Comrades, tonight you are leaving for the training camp: if you wish to be good soldiers in this fight, train well, learn well.'

We were told that the members of the Thaelmann Battalion were willing and anxious that the Englishmen should enter their ranks. We gave three cheers for Thaelmann and for the German comrades. Their leader replied: 'Three cheers for the English comrades who have come to fight with us.'†

The battalion was divided into companies, the companies into zugs of thirty men, and the zugs into groups of ten. With a dozen Flemings and a few Germans we formed the

* Kleber's real name was Lazar Stern and he was born in Bukovina, then part of Austria-Hungary. He served in the Austro-Hungarian army, was captured by the Russians and, like many other Jewish Austro-Hungarians, adhered to the Russian Revolution. He thereafter worked for the Comintern or Red Army Intelligence. He was later shot in the purges of 1937–1938 in Russia.

† This Thaelmann battalion which Romilly now joined was a part of the XIIth International Brigade, which was actually the second such Brigade to be formed. The commander of the XIIth International Brigade was at this first stage the Hungarian communist writer Mata Zalka known as General Lukacz. The Brigade comprised 1,550 men.

54

3rd Zug of the 1st Company. The Zug leader was a tall, tough Prussian with a gangster-face, called Paul, and above him was the Company Commander, Max, smaller and tidier and less shaggy, but even more of a Prussian. Jeans was our interpreter. He told us:

'Paul wants me to act as temporary leader of the English group in view of language difficulties. That is, if everyone is willing. . . .' There were a few murmurs, but everyone was willing, it seemed. Jeans went on: 'We have to have two groups. Form up now so we shall know them.' Birch was leader of the second group, and Keith and Don and I managed to keep together. Jeans told us we would not draw our equipment until after supper. A thin drizzle had started and we marched half a mile through squelching mud to the huge kitchen where soup and meat was served at long trestle tables. There was a merry atmosphere, like the last day at school; Joe led the singing from our party. When we got to 'Tipperary', Chris said: 'For Christ's sake stop that stupid song, that's a bourgeois imperialist thing. D'you think German comrades are going to like that?' But they did like it, and always asked us to sing it. Chris was an Oxford student.

At supper there was another little incident. Don was drinking too much, and was inclined to throw more bread across the table than anyone else. As he poured out another glass, Jeans said: 'You are a fool, Donovan, you'll be quite drunk, you know. Tcha.' He reached out his hand and knocked the bottle of wine on the floor. Don threw his plate of meat and rice into Jeans's face. Apologies on all sides followed, but there was a strained atmosphere for some time afterwards. We did not leave that night after all.

In the morning we were fitted out with uniforms of thick khaki coats and brown corduroy trousers, rifles, belts, boots, socks, plates, knives, spoons, mugs, and every sort of underwear. The trousers were all one size, and that size an outsize, so we either swam and wallowed in them, or cut off as much as twenty inches of the legs. I was alarmed by all these possessions, and had quite enough to think about with keeping myself together. Before we left we added a blanket to our gear.

After a sweating march to the station, with my pack and blanket continually coming undone, we had to wait an hour before the train arrived. Finally five of us jammed into a small compartment. Don had procured two bottles of white wine and some meat rolls, so we settled down happily. Paul rapped on the doors and shouted furiously in German. We smiled, so Jeans came back to interpret the message that anyone who was drunk from now on would be shot. Jeans was rather apologetic about it all, and said he thought his presence seemed to stir Don up so much that next time he'd send Birch along to give the orders. I went out and talked to Birch in the passage. 'It's perfectly ridiculous the fuss Don's making,' he said.

We reached the little town of Villa Franca at six in the morning. The last part of the journey I spent in wondering how I should ever be able to button myself up and get all my stuff together when we reached our destination. I was all right. Keith was not. His vital point gave way, that is, the buckle of the belt. Once that goes, munition pouches slide off the belt, shoulder straps come off the shoulders, your trousers come down, you must either let them fall or drop your rifle. All this happened to Keith. Don and I sweated hard to piece him together, but by the time we were ready the rest of the company had marched off to the barracks.

After breakfast Tich gave us instruction about our rifles. Jeans said to him: 'You know all about this, Tich, don't you?' Tich said: 'In the British Army, of course, you'd have a complete series of lessons on care of arms, first one simply to show you how to keep your rifle clean,' and when we asked him about this he told us, 'If you were in the trenches, say, an hour before stand-to in the morning, they'd have a rifle inspection, and those men who hadn't got their rifles cleaned would miss their rum rations.'

My chief difficulty was with the firing pin – every time I tried to push it up it shot out and bruised my thumb, and I was relieved when Tich said: 'Better leave that alone, son, you don't want to muck that about with oil and stuff.' Birch protested and argued that it was necessary to grease the firing pin, but personally I never once took my rifle to bits after this.

At eleven o'clock we marched through the little town to a piece of flat ground in the hills above. The town was all narrow, cobbled, muddy streets, with old men and children staring vacantly at us. When we halted, Jeans told us that we were going to practise various manoeuvres, that one of the officers present had been a colonel in the Reichswehr, that he would teach us the very latest German army tactics.

A difficulty soon cropped up, that it appeared he was the only man who knew them. The secret of it all was the triangular arrow-shaped formation – the battalion would be split like this, for attacking, then the companies and so on down to units of three. There was another division as well – out of each group of ten, half would be a light-machine-gun squad, and the rest would be in advance of the squad protecting it, and covering it with rifle fire. We practised for an hour or two at these manoeuvres.

'What about enemy tanks?' asked somebody. 'Get as close to them as possible!' was the answer.

The 'manoeuvres' (which always broke down because of bad co-ordination and because we could never understand the general plan) stopped abruptly when a motor-cyclist arrived at breathless speed to give a message to Max. Max told us:

'I am sorry. I wanted all of you to have a thorough training, for sixteen days at least. I am sorry. We are leaving at once for the front' (cheers interrupted him at this point). 'You will go in lorries. We do not know where the enemy is. If the lorries stop, get out at once, go into the nearest house, and stand ready.'

My only feeling, as this message was interpreted, was one of excitement. The one prospect I disliked was that of 'training'. But my spirits sank when we started. They sank because I had another violent attack of diarrhoea. We were cramped together – over twenty men with full equipment, in lorries meant for a maximum of fifteen – unable to stretch out and lie down, rocked about by the bad road, with a cold biting wind as an additional assault on my stomach.

My face must have gone very green, because someone leaned forward to ask Paul, who was sitting in front with the driver, to change places with me. It was better in front. Before we started they had distributed tins of fish and bread and pomegranates and the stink of all this food made me vomit.

As far as I could see on the road in front of us and behind was an endless stream of lorries; as we raced through the little villages on the way, crowds of old men and women and little girls collected in the squares. *'Salud! Salud!'* they shouted. *'Salud! No Pasarán! No Pasarán!'* It was a moving sight, but I was too occupied with my stomach to take any part in the frenzied cheering. At last I could contain myself no longer. The driver stopped at the side of the road, and lorries roared past. Half an hour later the driver stopped for me again near a farm-house. Six times altogether, I stopped on that journey.

At the back of the lorry the high spirits with which we had set off sank with the afternoon sun; when the lorries went on in the chilly night, everyone was cramped, tired, frozen and complaining. The 'Flemish comrades' had drunk large quantities of wine on the way, and one, in particular, a handsome, blue-eyed, blond young man, was sprawling over the floor, adding to the discomfort. The instructions regarding the imminence of the enemy were forgotten (this was as well, as they were due to an error in translation), no one cared about anything save the cold and discomfort. It was nearly midnight when we reached the straggling little market town of Chinchon. The lorries halted and disgorged their weary loads. In the darkness, packs and rifles and blankets were lost and confused. I turned over a bundle of equipment at the side of a road that I thought was mine. 'Don't you touch that, you b—,' I heard. Eventually I found my own stuff. We waited half an hour in the street. 'For Christ's sake, do something,' said Keith. 'Who's coming along to find ourselves some billets and get in them right now? I'm not going any farther tonight. There's a house that'll do.' 'Don't you do anything of the sort,' this was Tich's quiet authoritative voice, 'This is an army, my lad. You can go if you like, but I should think everyone else would have the sense to stay here and wait till Jeans come back.'

They found us a house. 'I've got a bed,' said Keith. 'A hammock kind of affair I found inside there. If you're feeling ill, you'd better have it.'

'I'm all right,' I said. 'I've got my stuff laid out on the floor. I'll be all right.' Then I had to dash out again, across the road to a smoky little café where men were drinking anis. I rushed in there, carrying my rifle, so as to be sure not to lose it when I got back, and stammered to the men behind:

'Donde esta el excus – el excusado?' When I came out, they made me some hot milk and gave me a lot of sympathy, which made me feel better. We slept about two hours. At three in the morning they woke us up, and we tramped down to the square to get into the lorries again. I saw Birch frenziedly arguing with a box of ammunition in his hand. Jeans was next to him, saying: 'But it should have all been brought down. Christ knows how we are going to distribute it!' We marched back to our billets, and they gave us 150 rounds apiece. The cartridges were stuffed into bandoliers, so that meant another difficulty getting them to fit into the pouches. Then they wanted us to take extra bandoliers of fifty cartridges to sling over our shoulders. 'Can't have too much of this stuff,' said Joe. 'Might need it, you know.' He was laden up like a hedgehog. I had quite enough without any more. I could imagine nothing worse than carrying more lead on me. In the lorry they distributed raw ham. There was nothing to drink. Jeans explained it to us:

'It is all simple; it's not that they don't want to give us proper food. Now I just hear the transport and food lorry is on the way; they went to the wrong place; there has been a sabotage somewhere in the Spanish high command. That is

59

why nothing was ready for us. They did not know we were coming. When we reach the front, we shall have proper food.'

Max made a speech. I could only catch a few words: '*Genossen, Genossen, allen treuen!*' They told us this was to be a big infantry engagement – we would have the Poles on our right and Spaniards on our left. In the lorry men were exchanging addresses of sisters, mother, wives; it was difficult not to feel a little dramatic. Keith said to me: 'You keep your head down; leave the shooting to the others.'

But it was a false alarm. We returned to our billets at five o'clock and slept soundly that night on the stone floor.

Next morning I felt better. I saw Norman at the wash-basins at ten o'clock, and we greeted each other heartily. 'Papers arrived yet?' he asked. Later on that day he and Keith and I went to drink anis in a little café in the square. Norman was cheerful and cynical. He taught us to sing, 'You're in the army now, O you're in the army now.' 'Stupid business, war,' he commented. 'Sitting in a trench, popping your head over the top and getting a bit of lead in it.' We had a third glass of anis, they were only ten centimos each. He whistled, and went on, 'I wouldn't mind seeing a nice Imperial Airways plane just taking off there, and a first-class ticket to Croydon, and then a damned good London fog.'

That day the word 'discipline' was everywhere. When we talked things over after lunch, Bill said: 'Now I'll tell you my impressions, lads, for what they're worth. They're these. It seems to me Paul and the rest of the German comrades have accepted us, but they're not going to stand for any disobedience of orders or larking about from the English group.'

'It's Prussianism,' said Keith, but he was in a minority.

At supper I had a talk with Chris. I liked him least of the whole group, but he said: 'I see quite well the chief difficulty everyone has is to get on with comrades they don't like; it's always bound to be a difficulty.' We talked a good deal about this, and I liked him more.

Before I went to bed, Marshall gave me a hair-cut; I

felt better after it. We asked Jeans if he thought there would be an alarm that night. 'Practically certain not,' he told us, though anything was possible. Jeans was working nearly a twenty-four hour day, disappearing for conferences with the staff, then doing an hour's interpreting in German or Polish or Yugoslavian. He looked tired but efficient. That night he shared a little ante-room with Keith and me. There was a crucifix over the wall and a dozen candles buried under the mat – those were the main things about that room.

Chapter 5

The bed on the floor was comfortable. I realized this fact at the same time as I realized it was still the middle of the night and a lot of noise was going on in the next room. Keith looked like an old witch. We both had only one thought – to get our equipment on efficiently. The first part was easy – general buttoning up everywhere and pulling on of sweaters and coat. Then the belt; this bit was more doubtful, it might have been better to get both shoulder straps on and then clasp the belt together as the final thing; but if you did this, there was always the danger of the ammunition pouches slipping off. Next step now was the trickiest of all. The shoulder straps were all ready attached to the three pouches, back and front, and I tried to slip into them like a pair of braces which has been left buttoned on to one's trousers. This was my first set-back; a general tightness everywhere made the action impossible, I had to detach them from the pouches and get Keith to do up the one at the back. Marshall had come in and helped to make things more cheerful, then Jock: 'Gracious me, are ye no ready yet? The fascists won't wait.'

'For Christ's sake get out of the way, Jock,' said Keith. 'If you want to be useful roll up those blankets instead of starting witty conversation.'

'Ye can roll up yer own f— blanket, and be f—.' As usual when Jock's sentences ended like this (and most of them did), the last two words were pronounced in a semi-spit with both lips protruding outwards.

I got my blanket spread out on the floor and we rolled it into a sausage; I was glad mine was done first, as it meant

Keith at any rate would be behind me. Fortunately I found a piece of cord at once in my pocket, and while Keith held the blanket I did up the ends. This was often a bad obstacle in getting ready, as I would have nothing handy, and would have to wait till the rest of my stuff was ready, and then look about for some old bootlace that could be used. Most people wrapped their blanket in a neat ball round their haversack, and slung the two together over their back. The only time I tried this method it kept on coming undone, and also it made a very heavy weight in one part; so I always used to carry it separately over my left shoulder.

When we were quite ready and I'd made certain I had the proper rifle, things looked brighter. My worrying period was over. We fell in outside the barracks. It was very cold. There was the usual shuffling about till everyone was in the proper group and zug. Ray and Lorrimer were struggling with the light machine-gun and having rather a job finding volunteers to carry the ammunition. I wished I'd been one of them, though, when Jeans called out two people and they came back staggering under the load of square boxes of rifle ammunition. Keith and I got one between us; any way you carried it it was bloody. The rope handle was worn thin so that this cut into your hands, alternatively if you gripped it where the top had been opened you were holding a piece of jagged metal. Best of all, really, was for one person to carry it on his shoulder, but it was a terrific weight and required someone else's help to hoist it up.

We walked a quarter of a mile to the place where hot coffee with brandy, bread and hunks of raw ham were dished out. There was a long wait, and I noticed Messer wasn't there. Norman told me he'd got bad toothache and had stayed behind as a guard on the building. Jock began to sing; originality wasn't his strong point and this was a familiar song about a hero who laid a damsel on the floor, and — as she'd never had before. Joe, as usual, was heavily equipped with pots and pans of every description. ('May need these, boy; might not get a bit of hot food for days.')

Norman told stories of two hens, and then sang a very funny ballad of how, on a hot and sultry afternoon, a stranger walked into a bar and proved more than a match for the barmaid, though she was famous for her prowess as the champion of the district. I liked Norman.

We assembled outside, and Hans Beimler was introduced as the political commandant of the Thaelmann Battalion.* He made a speech which Jeans translated, sentence by sentence; I noticed again how two solitary front teeth gave a humorous twist to everything he said. Beimler told us of the part he had played as a revolutionary leader in Germany, of his qualifications for the post he was to fill. His record was impressive; I put him immediately in my mind into the category of Real Communists. This was a purely personal definition I applied instinctively; to fit it you had to be a serious person, a rigid disciplinarian, a member of the Communist Party, interested in all the technical aspects of warfare, and lacking in any such selfish motive as fear or reckless courage.

Someone looked at his watch. It was ten minutes to three.

We marched off again, and it seemed to me we were going all over the town; we never seemed to get to our destination and I remember thinking to myself how much better it would have been if we had got straight into the lorries after eating. Going up a hill my thoughts were centred on one thing – the box of ammunition we were carrying. I tried and failed to get it on to my shoulder. Keith tried – and failed. Just then a pair of hands from behind gripped it. It was the original drunken Flem. He hoisted it on to his shoulder. I have never seen anyone so strong. The box was nothing to him; he laughed and joked all the way with it, paying no attention to our somewhat half-hearted attempts to take it from him. He was wonderful.

We reached the square where the lorries were waiting. As

* Hans Beimler (1895–1936) was a deputy in the Reichstag before 1933. Arrested by the Nazis, he escaped from Dachau and made his way to Spain via Moscow.

before, there was not nearly enough room. Jeans and Ray and Keith and I were parted from the rest, and got into a lorry with the second zug; I was lucky in getting a seat near the front where I had something behind me to rest on. There were twenty-four people in our lorry, all bulging with blankets and ammunition pouches, and all tripping over each other's bayonets and cursing. Those in the middle were worst off, as they had to rely on their neighbours' kindness to take a rest from sitting upright. We might have made ourselves quite comfortable if all the rifles had been stacked in one corner and haversacks in another; and we might have been quite warm if half a dozen people had spread out their blankets. But we didn't know when we'd be arriving and no one was willing to risk 'undoing' himself to that extent.

The day before, when we had turned out for a false alarm, I had felt – and most of us had felt – somewhat melodramatic at the idea of going to the front for the first time. Now that we were really off, I was occupied entirely with thoughts of personal comfort – of my back (whether it might not be better to take off my haversack and use it as a pillow), anxiety that my belt might burst, pre-occupation with the thought of keeping an eye on my rifle.

When we'd been going about half an hour the buckle of my belt did burst, and I struggled feverishly to hold its load together while I tried to do it up. It was hopeless. Jeans lent me a very old thin leather strap to use in its place, which I felt sure would break under the strain of the heavy weight. I stood up to readjust everything, and a sudden jerk caused my bayonet and two pouches to slip off the belt and fall into the road. I felt as though I had sustained a major disaster. It was picked up. I gradually dropped off to sleep, getting my head under a convenient pair of legs to escape the biting cold.

We reached our destination, the village of Melilla,* at nine o'clock. It was a beautiful sunny morning. Rest and warmth

* Assumed name. Apparently Villaconejos. It is not quite clear why Romilly should have disguised this.

had been the dominant ideas of everyone during the night, and driven out of our minds speculations as to the morning. If I was asked before what I thought going to the front would be like, I should have had to admit I hadn't the slightest idea. Certainly I hadn't envisaged arriving at a quiet country village on a sunny morning. We got out, stretching our legs, and found the remainder of the English.

There was a rest for half an hour on a little road winding out of the village. The country was hilly, resembling parts of the Sussex Downs. The machine-gun team consisted of five people – one fired, one loaded, one brought up more ammunition as it was needed, the other two were to keep always twenty yards in front to protect it with rifle fire. I was one of these two, Birch fired, Ray loaded, Marshall brought up the ammunition, and Chris was with me. This was how it was all planned out. Everyone asked questions. Jeans got a map and we grouped round to find out what was going to happen.

Just now we heard the first sounds of war; it was quite a pleasant noise, the dull thudding sound of artillery fire in the distance. Four tanks lumbered up the road, and we got into the ditch to let them pass. They looked rather ramshackle and were covered with branches of trees for camouflage; they were mounted with guns with long snouts, known as 'pom-poms' because of the noise they made firing.

'We have to attack a village over there and take it this morning,' said Jeans. 'The fascists may be in the farm-houses on the way. Our flyers who were reconnoitring yesterday saw no one, but they may have come up in the night. The Edgar André Battalion* are advancing along the river, and they will reach this village at the same time as us. The tanks are going along this road; they will go slowly so we can keep up with them.'

'Where is this village?'

* Another battalion of chiefly German communists called after Edgar André (1894–1936), a German communist executed by Hitler a month previously. To this battalion was attached an English machine-gun group which included the poet, John Cornford.

'Do we go straight along this road, then, behind these tanks, or what?'

'How far is this village?'

'How about us three in the other group. Do we get our orders from the Flems or what?'

'Where's this river?'

'Where on earth are we, anyway?'

'D'you know if we get any rations before we start? We haven't had anything since that stuff at Chinchon.'

'Is the whole battalion taking part in this, or just our company?'

All these hurried inquiries ceased as we heard the drone of aeroplane engines.

'*Fliege, Decke!*' (This warning of approaching planes soon became a familiar phrase in our vocabulary.)

We scrambled to separate and threw ourselves down under the trees. But the planes came nowhere near us. There were three of them. They made three circles, and each time at the same point on the circumference there were three bursts of smoke; it was a beautiful sight; it looked not at all terrifying, but strangely peaceful. Jeans had been called away for a conference with Paul.

'Our aeroplanes bombing the enemy positions,' he said when he came back.

Norman and Don were detailed to follow behind with the ammunition (I didn't envy them that job!); the rest of us left the road and began to advance; we were in the V-shaped formation we had practised at Villa Franca. The hills became higher ahead of us, so we had ample cover. But we advanced cautiously, stopping and lying flat down every ten yards. I was between Ray and Marshall, who kept a bit behind, and Bill Scott was level with me a few yards to the right. We kept on stopping to see that everyone was properly in formation, and that there was liaison on both sides with the other zugs.

The sun was getting very hot. We had left our blankets and haversacks at our starting-point. After we had been going half an hour, up and down the rises, we turned round and came back, as it appeared we had been going in the wrong direction.

'Everyone to take all equipment,' said Jeans.

We set off, walking in three lines this time, or rather stumbling. The heat was stifling. Everyone was in a bad temper. I wondered if we should always have to fight carrying blankets and haversacks. Everything on me seemed to be slipping – shoulder straps, belt, trousers and bandolier.

'I guess I'd like to know where I can hand in my resignation from this army.' It was Jerry, the little American.

I imagine this was all rather like an O.T.C. Field Day – very hot, exhausting and disagreeable. I wished I had brought a flask of water; but this would have meant something else to clank about my neck and get tied up in.

We rested for the laggards to join up with those in front. We were leaving the hills on the left and getting near the marshy ground near the river. We were lucky in avoiding the sweat of climbing, but we had exchanged this for the difficulties of a cross-country obstacle race, the obstacles being chiefly ploughed fields and hedges.

'I hope we don't have much more of this sort of war,' said Tich. He seemed bowed down by his gear, like a very small porter carrying a lot of heavy luggage.

Very soon we reached the main obstacle – the river (or rather a muddy stream). Jeans set an example by striding across first, but then he had huge rubber gum-boots; Babs had them too, and he followed. It was fortunate no one else did, as just then came word we shouldn't have crossed at all.

'Everybody should have a cartridge ready in the breech.' The order was passed from mouth to mouth.

'There may be machine-gun nests in the farm buildings ahead. When you get the word, everyone to run forward ten yards, then lie down, one at a time, starting from the right.'

This advance was achieved successfully, though Aussie, who had been tying up his boots and hadn't heard the instructions, was left behind, and someone had to go back and

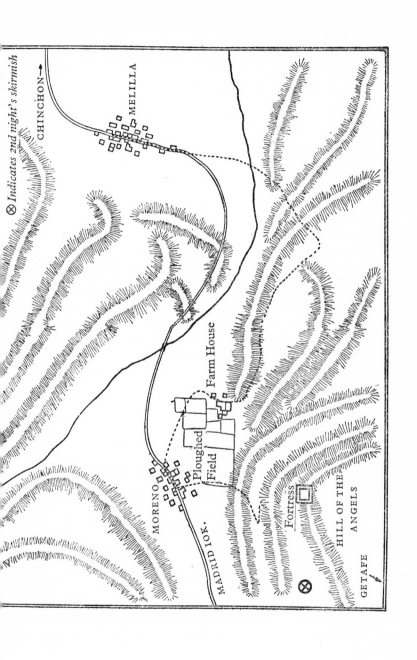

fetch him. There was still the Field Day atmosphere.

A quarter of a mile ahead, across three muddy fields, we could see the farm buildings. At first I kept my head well down before a piece of rising ground at the prospect of so imminent an enemy. But we were still thinking most of those blankets. In a few minutes people were walking about openly, keeping their heads down only as a formality for a minute at a time. Chris had got a flask of water, and at last I managed to secure it. I tipped it over till it was almost vertical, but still with no result.

'Don't drain it, man!' But there was nothing to drain.

I was nearest to Tich, and we did each other's straps up. One or two people had thrown their blankets away.

The Field Day went on for another hour. We captured first the farm buildings, then the village. In the first there wasn't a soul. In the second a mangy dog and a dead cat.

Exploring the houses, someone discovered bread and a half-eaten ham. Our efforts had been really crowned with success, for now we were able to take off blankets, haversacks ammunition and have a proper rest. What a glorious feeling of relief it was! I suppose a war is essential for proper appreciation of resting and doing nothing; there is an exquisite feeling of weary, tender relief on all the parts of the shoulders where cart-wheels have been made by straps; what a pleasure to differentiate the various forms of relief – relief from cutting straps, relief from bruising weights, relief from carrying, relief from moving.

I didn't notice much of the village – it was a collection of houses on the road. Written in faded characters on a wall at the corner was the inscription: NORENO,* and underneath an arrow and the words – Madrid, 10 kilometres.

I began to understand something of the action. Between Madrid and this village were the rebel lines. Our next move was the attack on the fortress. In Noreno we had several hundred men, all of the Thaelmann Battalion. Another force

* Assumed name.

was attacking from the farm; another from our original position in the hills facing it; another from the west, where we had seen the tanks going forward. (Incidentally, this was the last we saw of those tanks that day.)

Babs and Joe were arguing: 'Don't be so silly, course it's crazy trying to attack a fort – if that's what it is – without artillery. What d'you think you're going to do, knock on the front door and walk right in?'

'I expect they'll start bombarding it right away if we are going to attack this afternoon. Or it might be we're going to do a surprise night attack. Astonishing there's no tanks here, though, I must say.'

This was Tich, who had joined in. He was to be astonished many times in the course of the next months, but his quiet reassuring manner always had the effect, on me at any rate, of making one think that the organization of the British Army was really present all the time, and just a few mistakes only stopped it from being at once apparent.

Knowing nothing of war, nothing surprised me much in the way it was fought.

We parked blankets and haversacks in the village. I felt better this time, now I didn't have to concentrate on keeping myself together.

The sun was still hot when we left Noreno. Keith couldn't be found at all; he was hunting about in the hopes of finding a decent pair of boots in one of the houses. We went without him. We could see the fort when we had crossed one field; it seemed a long way off.

'Forward in lines, ten yards at a time!'

'Keep down, keep down, keep your heads down!'

This was something quite new, and in a second the Field Day was over.

Swish – Swish – Swish; it was like a cool breeze whistling through the grass; then quicker and nastier.

Swish – swish – swish – swish; they seemed to be rustling through the grass. We were in an open ploughed field. I worked like mad for several minutes, scrabbling up the earth

72

in front with my hands. I don't know how long I stayed in the same position; it might have been ten minutes or half an hour.

'Who's that in front, hi, there!'

I looked round, keeping my head well down. It was Bill Scott, about fifteen yards behind.

'This is a nasty spot to get caught,' he shouted. 'Who's that next to you?'

I shouted at the figure that was huddled up in the ground on my right. It was Jerry; he wasn't taking any chances by getting up to join in the conversation. I couldn't see anyone else from where I was, though I could hear voices in English and German. We waited for new orders. Just after the first enemy bullets a continual racket of firing had started over on our left. I began to feel cold.

'Think I'll have a pot,' shouted Bill, and the next moment I heard a deafening explosion. This was his pot; then came the clink of a breech being shoved home and another shot. It was far more disconcerting than the bullets over us, and I hoped he would soon stop. But it gave me an idea, and I decided myself to fire my first round.

'They're too far. You can't see a thing,' said Bill.

Taking a hasty glance over my earth mound to make sure where the fort was, I pointed my rifle at an angle of forty-five degrees, and pressed the trigger. The result was a click. Furious, I emptied the breech; but I had done everthing right and another clip of cartridges produced no result.

'I expect they'll as like find half these rifles are dud by the time the day's over,' said Bill.

We heard Jeans's voice calling us to get up and run to the edge of the field, where the rising ground gave cover. Everyone was there, all waiting, breathless from the exertion. It was four o'clock and beginning to get chilly. Being under fire wasn't as bad as I had expected; to lie flat down and feel the bullets passing overhead gave a curious feeling of security, as though one had found a new and powerful weapon of protection in the ground itself. But I didn't realize then that

what we had experienced was nothing – if I had known anything of war I should have known from the pleasant rustle
like wind – that the bullets came from so far as to be comparatively harmless. They had none of the deadly, wicked
twang of close-range fire.

For the moment I was preoccupied with anxiety to get my
rifle working before we advanced again. I gave it to Tich. He
extracted the firing pin, adjusted something, and told me it
would work all right now.

'Where did you get to?' asked Birch. (Bill and I had been
almost the last to leave the open field.)

'Goodness knows,' said Bill, 'whether we were the advance
guard or the rearguard. If you ask me, we were the only
people who were going in the right direction for the fort.'

This time I kept with the machine-gun group. We advanced
slowly – two men dashing forward at a time from one rough
piece of cover to another. It was all right at first, then it began
to get nasty, as the cover became scarcer. The nastiness took
a definite form. Previously, we had only heard the bullets
whistling through the air; now we could see them spattering
the earth around us when we lay flat on the ground. Just
behind me Birch was cursing with the light machine-gun.

'Ask Jeans if we're supposed to set this thing up each time
we stop.' The message was passed on, but the reply never
arrived, as just then came another order to advance.

Looking up, I was surprised to see the fortress more clearly.
We were now about three-quarters of a mile south-west of it,
but it seemed much nearer. On both sides, west and south-east
of the fort, came the flashes and explosions of rifle and
machine-gun fire. My dominant feeling was excitement – then
the smack of a bullet in the earth near me modified this feeling. Jeans trotted (that is the only way to describe someone
trying to run nimbly over a lot of obstacles carrying a good
load) back, with his head bent – he paid no attention to the
firing; everyone else was lying flat. He told us the fortress was
under the fire of our tanks on the west side, that the present
orders were for the machine-gun to be prepared for action in

74

a position for continual firing before it got too dark; the rest of us were to take up positions a few hundred yards ahead. I dug with my bayonet to make a position near the machine-gun. Just now, only a few stray bullets came our way. After a lot of clinking and arguing and cursing I heard the rat-tat-tat of our light machine-gun. We were all a bit surprised it worked.

'Good effort,' shouted Chris.

'The thing's too damned stiff,' cried Birch.

'Christ Almighty, man,' said Chris, looking round, 'you're firing at the sky, not the fort!'

'Rot!'

The effect of this fire was startling and disagreeable. We were suddenly in a hurricane of bullets. Birch went on a few minutes, then he and Ray and Marshall found it too hot to continue. I remembered I was supposed to be doing some 'protection'. Unfortunately, I could discern no figures at whom to direct my fire; I discharged five rounds, putting the sights at 1,000 metres – it was the first time I had fired a rifle in my life, but I had little time to reflect on the occasion; it seemed very unfair that the enemy now seemed to be able to see me but I could not see them.

There was a cry behind me. Ten yards behind the machine-gun two drums of ammunition lay on the ground, beside them was a German, clutching his leg and groaning.

Ray crawled back to him. The bullet had entered his left thigh. I went back to help; he was in great pain but was able to move. The firing had ceased and everything around was quiet.

'I'm all right,' he said. 'It's nothing, really.'

He stood on one leg with my arm supporting him round his back.

I went back, the wounded man hopping along under the support of my arm. It was dark. We could find no one, though at intervals I stopped and shouted: 'Sanitas! Sanitas!' For direction, I had no guide save an attempt to remember which way we had come and the general principle of getting farther from the fort – the outlines of which still stood out clearly in the dark. The German was tired and had to rest on the ground. His lip was covered in blood where he had bitten it to stop crying out with the pain of the wound. Just then I heard voices speaking in French. There were twenty of them, and they took the German back to Noreno, where there was sure to be a dressing station or transport to get back. They pointed out in which direction the village lay. I asked what had happened: one of them spoke very excitedly:

'We were round the other side. . . . My God; I tell you we were a bare 300 yards from the fort – and what happened? They fired at us from the other side – they were machine-gun bullets. There were six killed and we couldn't get the wounded back. Who was it firing? We don't know; it's terrible, we don't know anything – there's no organization, there's nothing. . . .'

I thought it would be an easy matter to return to our position, now I knew where everything was. After what seemed an hour, I had got nearer the fort, and that was all; there was not a sound, either of firing or voices. The moon had risen. I was positive I was now very near where our machine-gun had been placed. After another period of futile wandering, I had a sudden inspiration. In my mind I pictured the village as the south point of a compass and the fort as the north (this hadn't any relation to geography but it was the only way I could get the picture at all); now, I thought, we hadn't gone straight 'north' from the village at all, but diagonally in a 'north-east' direction. In that case, I was at the wrong corner of the fort altogether. I started walking confidently, but the confidence didn't last long; nothing was changed, except for a sudden awful thought which assailed me as I remembered the Frenchman's words. What if I had got right round the other side of the fort? What if. . ? It had never occurred to me before that since the operation we had taken part in was an attack, and since Noreno had been unoccupied or occupied by the enemy until our arrival, there might well be some of the enemy anywhere around me. I suppose I must have assumed that as we were attacking the fort, they would be staying in that fort. But that was ridiculous; they could not be in it unless they had lines of communication with their other forces – all the country on one side was theirs. Suppose I was in this country now? Then came a more welcome idea – perhaps the fort was captured already. But the Frenchman's account didn't give much encouragement to this idea.

I sat under a tree – that was only one realization that had just come to me; another was that I was cold and exhausted; another that I hadn't had food for a long time. But still the dominant feeling was that I must somehow find my group. This was the major calamity – being lost.

Then a miracle happened. I heard a noise of someone approaching, and the words: 'Is there anyone there?' They were spoken in English – the English of County Kerry, Ireland. Bill Scott was as glad to see me as I was to see him.

'Was that chap hurt bad?' he asked, 'We must have been a good way in front. You could see 'em – not very clear – moving about, I had a good many pots at them, but it was a lot too hot for my liking. Some German came up and shouted some order; I didn't catch what it was. . . .'

Bill was also lost. 'The others are back at that village, now. You can be sure,' he added, 'everything's been packed up for the night by the look of things. We'd better be pushing back ourselves.'

I heartily agreed, and was much cheered by the confident way in which Bill spoke of getting back. I was prepared to put myself entirely into his hands. It was so infinitely better to be with someone and I felt the situation was much brighter. Also I remembered my blanket was at Noreno, and there were houses there for warmth and rest.

We found neither blankets nor Noreno – and no rest or warmth that night either. First downgrade of my spirits came when I began to disagree with Bill's geography. We would walk briskly in one direction – then one of us would swear he had got it straight, it was slap the opposite way, and we would turn round with a new briskness; the briskness would flag and the process be repeated.

'Stars might be some use,' muttered Bill. 'Only you don't know which is north and which is south.'

Bill became more and more gloomy. 'Christ knows when we shan't run into a band of roving Moors,' was another of his reflections.

We stumbled into lines of deep-built trenches. I was in favour of getting into them, and resting a bit, but Bill drew such a picture of Moors and fascists returning at dawn – or any moment – to occupy what were obviously their positions that the prospect seemed less pleasant. Just then began the intermittent noise of artillery fire; whose it was or what its objective, we hadn't the slightest idea. It made everything more melodramatic; together with the trenches it made me think of stories of the Great War, and for the first time I realized that we were spending a night in No-Man's-Land during a modern war. To say the least, these trenches were very odd – almost ghostly in their emptiness; but old mess tins showed they must have been occupied recently.

We heard voices and listened intently to try to catch the language; if it was German or French, we should be all right. We left the trenches and approached cautiously in the direction of the sound of the voices. Then they grew fainter.

'They must be ours,' I said. Anything seemed better than this terrible suspense and aimless wandering. Besides, I thought, we must find someone by the time it's light.

'Sh – sh! You can hear now. What is it?'

It sounded like Italian; that would be the Garibaldi Battalion;* then again it might be Spanish – which side? There had been no Spanish troops, I was sure, in this action. It must be the fascists. Bill tugged at my arm. 'For Christ's sake, man! Don't let's go walking into a nest of fascists.' We returned and passed the trenches again. I was now sure we were going in a direction parallel with the road from Noreno

* The Garibaldi Battalion was in the same (XIIth) International Brigade as the Thaelmann Battalion, and was composed of Italians.

to Madrid, into enemy country. We sat down under a tree with our rifles ready. I felt far from heroic.

Another age passed. Then we saw lights approaching in the distance, two spots of brightness nosing their way forward.

'Must be a lorry or something,' said Bill. 'Means there's a road here, anyway.'

We found the road – or rather a muddy track – not more than a few hundred yards away, and lay down on the grass at the side. There was a whispered conference as to what we should do, and whose the lorry might be. It passed. We had done nothing. Two minutes later, as we watched it recede in the distance, four men came down the road from the same direction; they were talking – French, I could swear. We got up and walked towards them; thay appeared to be in a ragged condition like ourselves. I was peering all the time through the dark trying to make out their uniform; it was the same as ours.

'*Alto! Quien està?*' shouted one of them as we met. A mixture of ideas raced through my mind. I was sure they were our people – but not quite sure, the challenge in Spanish had started doubts. On the other hand the challenge didn't seem very serious, else they would surely not have walked on towards us when they first saw us, without taking some precautions; and nobody was pointing a rifle at us now. The challenge seemed rather the sudden idea of inquiry of one of them. We ignored it, nodded as though to pass it off as of no importance, and scrutinized them closely. They were French all right – and also lost.

Since I set out to find my group and zug, our forces had doubled and trebled. This process continued throughout the night until there were about fifty of us. As we grew stronger, there became less 'compromise' in our challenging and picking up the groups of two or three. Never did there come any sort of agreement as to where was 'home' and what it might consist of. Increasing numbers brought another feature to our relations to add to the disagreement – this was that half the men suspected the other half of being enemies, and only tiredness and general depression prevented them from saying so. It must be nearly day, I thought. Actually, it was three o'clock.

At last we found another road, where a party of thirty was sitting, or lying on the ground in the ditch, and there was a mass of machine-guns, drums and boxes of ammunition, and odd rifles stacked together. It was under the command of a German-Polish officer who had been given the job of collecting everyone who had lost his battalion. I remembered having seen him at Chinchon, talking with Van Renn* and Beimler; I thought he must belong to the Edgar André Battalion (also composed of Germans).

The first person I noticed there was Keith. He looked like a worried old nanny-goat; I said so, and all three of us forgot the depressing situation for half a minute and laughed. Keith, having been left behind at the beginning of the attack, had had an even more hectic time than we had.

'Have they captured the fort?' I asked.

'Captured it? They'll never take that place. I was with some of the French boys. God knows what they didn't leave behind. I don't wonder, seeing some crazy bastards started firing at them; they stuck it as long as they could. . . . The Flems over the other side got a few shells in them, and that was the last of them. They'd packed up by five o'clock.'

The commander shouted at Keith and Bill to carry a stretcher somewhere. It was the last I saw of them that night. I did not know any of the other men before; they were mostly French and Polish. We rested an hour and a half near the road, guards keeping a constant watch in all directions; less than half of us had blankets, but those who had them shared them out, so that two or three people slept under one. Surprisingly, it was possible to keep quite warm in this way: I slept.

It was still night when the order came to get up and prepare to move off. All the extra machine-guns and ammuni-

* Presumably Ludwig Renn, the German writer who was at this time the commander of the Thaelmann Battalion.

tion had to be taken with us. This meant you carried something heavy and unpleasant for as long as possible, then handed it on to someone who had nothing. We went along the road and at first kept roughly in ranks of three; after a time there were no more ranks and the column straggled over half a mile.

At the time, I did not know that we were returning to Melilla on the main road, that curved round the hills from Noreno. The distance was six miles. Often the order would come for those in front to stop and the stragglers would come up. Many people, unable to carry on, lay down in the ditch at the side; then followed on at the end. Everywhere I was a mass of aches and pains; but after an hour I no longer felt the pain in different parts of my body, but just a general numbness, almost a dizziness. I remembered that same feeling of tingling dizziness once at the end of a long cross-country run four years before, coming down the long avenue of the grounds of Wellington College. It seemed I wasn't the same person now – I had different senses and feelings, if any at all; perhaps I could go on for ever like this.

When we reached Melilla (I still had no idea I had ever seen this village before), there was a long wait, while accommodation was found. I had made friends with two Norwegian boys who spoke English; one of them had a blanket, and offered me its hospitality when they found us somewhere to sleep. The stars and moon had disappeared, it would soon be light. We got a crowded stone floor to sleep on in the end; we kept our equipment on, which made us fatter and bulgier and less easy for the blanket to cover.

Chapter 6

It was light, and men scrambled out of the window to find their battalions. I was worried to see no English or Germans anywhere; I felt I had been thoroughly inefficient in getting lost, and longed for a chance to redeem myself.

Then I saw Jeans's head, at the window.

'Let's go along and see if we can find something to eat,' he said. It appeared that eight people – out of fourteen – were missing. I suppose I should have been anxious for their safety. I wasn't. I was profoundly relieved to hear I hadn't been the only one to get 'lost'. The possibility that any of them might have been killed or wounded I ruled out. I wasn't thinking of 'war' but rather of a situation where I must try and do the right thing and not be conspicuous by reason of my inefficiency.

We could find nothing to eat. Jeans picked up an old chunk of bread off the ground and we ate this. It was covered with a thin layer of frosty dew on one side.

The missing people began to turn up. Joe and Tich and Babs had spent an excellent night in beds with sheets and warm blankets in the farm-house we had 'captured' near the village.

'Oh, boy,' Joe shouted so that everyone could hear his luck, 'nothing to grumble about there! Spaniards there, there were, half a dozen of them, all young chaps you know. I think they thought we were fascists at first, but I said "Genossen" and "Camaradas" and they soon twigged. Asked us if we were hungry, and we sat down to fried eggs and coffee!'

This description was more than we could stand for.

Other impressions were: Chris: 'This is bloody flu, I've got.'

Birch: 'I wish we'd made that night attack Paul was talking about.'

Jerry: 'I guessed it was night all right when that sun said good-bye.'

The sun had now risen again and done much to cheer our spirits. Most of that day we spent lying about in different positions on the hills outside the village, whence we had started the attack the day before. Lorries with rations came up, and we had generous supplies of hard-boiled eggs, bread, butter, tinned meat, wine and coffee; also there was any number of pomegranates; I sucked at least twelve of these. The village looked like the Sussex Downs during the visit of a party of trippers. The big event of the day was an air-raid, at about midday.

Once more we saw Noreno bombed; once more it was a magnificent sight, three planes circling over it, only this time they were enemy bombers. *'Fliege, Decke!'* had been shouted at the first sound of the engines, and we had made haste to conceal the blankets and tins that were lying about. Bill and Keith and Don and Norman were still missing – it occurred to us now they would almost certainly be in Noreno. The planes disappeared; ten minutes later we heard their drone again; now they were right overhead. When they dropped their bombs on Melilla the explosion and vibration of the ground were tremendous. We were all together in a group.

'We oughtn't to be like this, all bunched up together,' shouted somebody.

'Still! Still! Keep quiet!' It was Paul's voice, frenziedly trying to attract the attention of several people who were running about.

The planes had turned round; they were coming back overhead, now they were right on top of us. Lying flat down, my face pressed against the ground, I instinctively clasped my head with my hands for protection. I heard a long, shrill whistle, then Boum, Boum, Boum! Three gigantic smacks, each seeming louder than the last; there could not have been half a second between the first and third crash. I lay quite still. Surely we couldn't have survived it. Then I heard Jerry:

'God damn it. Those chaps up there, they see they've missed us, and they're coming back. . . . I'm not needing company next time.' He ran to a tree a few hundred yards away.

But the raid was over, and we were able to take stock of its results. No one was hurt, though four or five people had been showered with earth and sticks and stones; a huge hole in the ground showed where one of the bombs had fallen fifty yards away. In the village, one bomb had fallen in the street, another in an improvised hospital where four people had been killed and ten wounded. I asked Birch what the planes were like. With more courage than I, he had watched them all the time till the little gleams of silver whistled downwards. They were big German Junkers, the swastikas on their tails clearly visible though they flew at a good height.

Soon afterwards Bill turned up. His face had been cut by broken glass when Noreno was bombed. He and Keith had stayed the night at a house in the village, and the bombs had fallen in the street outside. Keith had been taken back by ambulance, he thought; he himself had come back with some Frenchmen in a lorry and he thought Noreno was now evacuated. Donovan had gone back wounded. Norman was still missing.

All day we watched shells bursting round the fort, with now and then a direct hit. We were constantly getting into different positions to be ready if there was an attack, so we never got a chance to sleep in the sun.

In the evening, we prepared for a night attack. We marched a mile down the now familiar road. I was next to Aussie and Jerry; Aussie lent me his mac to wear, as it was very cold and I had neither coat nor blanket. Sid had lost most the day before – having turned up minus coat, jacket, rifle and ammunition. (The last two items had been replaced.)

Aussie was expounding philosophy in his jerky manner.

'Does a man good in some ways, a battle,' he was saying. 'Don't matter who a man is or where he comes from. He might have been to Oxford or he might be a tramp: a man like me that's picked up his own education. But it's all the same here, when you might get killed the next moment. . . . This is a good bunch, though, I'll say that, it's a good thing to stick around with a bunch like this when you get in a tough spot.'

We left the road, to the left; though I did not realize it, this was practically the same country as we had crossed yesterday. We learned now that there was no plan to attack the fort; tonight we were expected to settle with any enemy patrols between Noreno and Melilla. Noreno had been evacuated by our forces in the morning for two reasons: by advancing on to a crest a few hundred yards from the fort the fascists had the road under the fire of their machine-guns; also concentrations of enemy troops had been observed advancing across country from the north (that is, from the direction of Madrid). All day we had been in readiness for a direct infantry attack, of which the air-raid might well have been the prelude. Patrols had kept watch in the hills overlooking Noreno and facing the fort; but the fascists had shown no signs of entering the village; what effect the artillery bombardment of the fort might have had was unknown. Our job tonight was to 'establish contact' with the enemy.

We were acting as zugs, each unit being about thirty men, each striking out in a different direction. Liaison was difficult in the event of resistance being encountered during an advance by any of these units. It was arranged for the words '*Viva la*' to be shouted as a challenge, with the word '*Republica*' as the reply. A Spanish column was to reach Noreno and send patrols forward on the Madrid road.

We had a quiet time the first part of the night. We would advance a bit, then settle down in our blankets and sleep with two sentries posted. That is, those who had blankets did so. Birch and Ray and Sid and myself found ourselves out in the cold. Occasionally we tried to get in under Joe's, but his temper was bad over a quarrel he had had with the Germans over the rations.

'If we all hunch ourselves up, facing the same direction, one behind the other, it'll be all right,' said Birch. 'Sid's so big he can go on the outside.'

I got between him and Sid. Sid was whistling and grumbling from the cold wind which lashed his front. Theoretically, I should have been the best off in the middle, but odd bits of arm and leg and ear kept getting frozen. Our next rest, I got under Harry's blanket. In the middle of this, they dished out stew and coffee. I realized I should have done better to keep my spoon and mess tin, as by the time I borrowed one, the stew was cold and greasy. Joe was best off here, as he had come out of the action with all his pots and forks and spoons still hanging on his belt.

I never managed to keep any of my stuff together. Fortunately, losable objects like belts and bayonets and plates could be found anywhere – abandoned by someone else. The blanket was the thing I determined to keep at all costs; the sweat of carrying it in the boiling sun was nothing compared with the misery of being without it at night.

At three o'clock we rested before climbing a crest. As we neared the top, the order was given for absolute silence. Then: 'Everyone ready, lie down in firing positions,' was whispered by Jeans.

The crest was a natural trench. Peering over, I saw at first only the sky; then raising my head higher and looking around I made out the outlines of a building behind us to the left. We had left the fort behind us.

Excited whispers broke out.

'Do you see those people?'

'Where?'

'Down there.'

'Can't see anything.'

'Look, now! Quick!'

'Don't be so silly, a couple of stray horses, that's all that is.'

86

'Sh – now! Quiet!'

We could all see clearly now. It was a clear night, the moon was almost full and the crest we were on commanded many lower ridges ahead. What we saw came suddenly out of the obscurity on to a piece of high ground. One, two, three men – on horseback, they were trotting towards us; then another three. Their red caps stood out in the night. Someone whispered: 'Moors!' They seemed very close, but our high position made the distance deceiving; now the first lot were almost out of sight under the ridge. Two Germans peered right over to see which way they went. They had wheeled round to the right along a path that went along the bottom of the ridge. Half a mile to our right this path turned sharp right again, running between our ridge and another. The second zug was on this other ridge. We counted eighteen of them in groups of three; each group was about fifty yards apart.

At the bottom of our ridge, all but the first three halted. These went right on down the path. No one whispered or moved. We were waiting in breathless excitement, hoping they would see and hear nothing. After an interminable wait, the order was whispered for the English group to remain while the rest of the zug went over to the right. We were told the whole Moorish patrol had gone on.

'Shoot, and let 'em have it hot and strong the first black face you see. That's the idea, boy,' whispered Joe.

'You fire before you get the order, you'll muck the whole thing up,' said Tich, who heard the remark.

' 'Course you will, you great crazy blighter,' Babs supported his friend.

The stillness was broken by a crash, then three more at intervals of ten seconds. Half a minute's silence, then a continuous racket broke out and the hills were ablaze with the flashing of rifle fire. The contrast with the stillness before was amazing, it was like an inferno. It went on for ten minutes, an occasional bullet going over us. Then the firing became more desultory. We had scrambled right on to the top of the ridge, ready to pour lead into anyone we saw returning down the path. A riderless horse galloped back; several rounds were fired before we realized what it was. It went through all the bullets, following the path all the way.

'They won't come back this way at all now; they'll get back over the hills,' said Jeans.

Actually we saw four without their horses. I could have sworn my cartridge had got one of them, but then, everyone afterwards claimed dozens of victims. It is fairly certain all four were killed. Joe wanted to go and catch two horses we saw, but was not allowed to. Having 'established contact' with the enemy, we now withdrew hastily. Our withdrawal was made difficult by the second zug, who, flushed with their success with the Moors, opened rapid fire on us for a time. No one was hurt.

We spent the next two days in a quarry; this was half a mile from the fort (not, however, on the enemy's side where we had met the Moors). Tich now came much more to the front, being the only one who knew anything about making our position safe. He was also unanimously elected provisioner, being in charge of rationing out all the food and appointing people to fetch it. This was a heavy job, as the food lorries were a quarter of an hour's walk away. At this time, rations were given out at irregular intervals, but there was at least one hot meal of stew a day. That is, it started by being hot, though by the time it arrived, it and the coffee were nearly always cold.

Our quarry was shared with the Flems – they were very heavy eaters; relations between us got rather luke-warm over the food question.

Joe made up for the deficiency by his own private efforts. Since the supply was none too good, private enterprise often took its place in the distribution of supplies. The word used for this form of supplying was to 'organize'. One was always 'organizing' extra tins of meat, or 'organizing' extra blankets, or 'organizing' cooking implements. Birch was the only person really against the principle of 'organizing'; Jeans and Tich and Ray were at first, but they, like everyone, approved of 'organizing' on behalf of the group.

Air bombing was frequent those three days. You could be fairly certain that a rest in the sun would not last long, before you would be rudely awakened to hide everything and yourself from sight. One took place while Jerry and I had gone to get rations. Near the food lorry were strewn hundreds of bright tins, and several coffee containers which reflected the sun. The men dishing out the stuff ran away from this as quickly as they could, as did everyone else who was drawing rations. Jerry and I had the same idea: bombers hardly ever made a direct hit on their objective, usually the bombs fell several hundred yards away; they would see all the tins and perhaps the lorry, aim at it and miss it. Meanwhile, we would get hold of a sack and pack in a liberal quantity of goods, and get a hero's welcome when we returned. Actually, no bombs were dropped within five miles of the lorry, so our plan worked excellently. The coffee pot we carried on a pole, each holding an end, and this, with all the food in the sack, and our pockets bulging with extra hard-boiled eggs and pomegranates, made a terrific load. Our effort was wasted, because before we got back to the front, Ray met us to say we were retiring. Most of the food had to be abandoned.

Every kind of explanation was given for the order to retire, such as strong attacks expected, and orders for a retreat of ten kilometres to better positions. Actually, we were being relieved. The night before there had been none of the usual 'strafing' from the fort; it had been evacuated by the fascists. The Thaelmann Battalion, we were told officially by Max, was to return to Chinchon for reorganization. On the drive back, twenty miles through a beautiful countryside, everyone was in excellent spirits. However much anyone may have enjoyed the front, the moment of leaving the front line, of the thought of comfort and warmth and absence of bullets is always welcome.

In Melilla we saw the new troops – all Spanish – who were taking our place. We left in an atmosphere of shouting, cheering and friendly words. In the lorry, Jeans and I each had a supply of pomegranates, which we shared out. The Flems had got wine and were soon drunk once more, but our differences were forgotten when Joe produced two tins of bully beef, exclaiming: 'Here, Flemish genossen, you take these; *is fleisch, gut!*' I began to like Jeans much more. He told me he had once tried to learn French in addition to the other languages he spoke; he stayed at a pension in the Midi, but all the people there were Russian refugees, and so he had learned no French at all.

Back at the barracks at Chinchon, Birch and I made up a joint bed for extra warmth with two macintoshes as mattress and our blankets and coats as covering. We argued a bit about Keith and Norman. Bill had now told us he didn't think after all Keith had been wounded. In the course of the argument, Birch admitted he had only tried to get on with him on principle. Birch had a lot of principles.

'I was very sorry to see you seemed to be under his influence,' he said.

'Rot,' I answered. 'Do you mean you object to him merely because he has a sense of humour and isn't as much a communist as you are?'

'I mean because of his whole attitude and behaviour, not his opinions. You haven't known him as long as us.'

I was annoyed with Birch for taking the line that I had fallen under anyone's influence, but glad of the friendship the remark showed. Norman had not turned up either on the morning after the first action.

When we went into the town, Jeans said, 'Paul won't have any more to do with this zug if Keith and Norman come back at any time and try to rejoin us.' Both had been particular friends of mine, but I took their exit very much for granted; I suppose because the conditions we were in made one adaptable to any change of one's friends or one's circumstances. Then we spoke no more of them, but had a lot of wine, got suitably drunk, and felt were we all behaving as people just returned from the front should behave.

Chapter 7

We had a Group Meeting at Chinchon. All this didn't seem so important now; you were inclined to be annoyed with the interruption if you were cleaning your rifle or getting your possessions together. Bill was chairman. The first point of discussion was whether there should have been a Group Meeting at all in the first place.

'I feel every comrade should think seriously about this question,' said Bill. 'When Max made the announcement we were leaving for Madrid, he expressly stated he favoured discussion of the change of plans. If we don't discuss this kind of thing, we might as well be fascists.... A lot of comrades probably feel we were entitled to a proper rest back here as we were promised.'

Birch was furious at the thing being discussed, and said it would give us a bad reputation among the Germans. Jeans looked tired and said little. He had come to interpret to us the new orders about leaving for Madrid. Tich was pleased because Max had announced that we would be fighting in properly-constructed trenches. Sidney caused some trouble by not attending to the proceedings.

'I don't think,' said Bill, 'that Comrade Sid can contribute anything to this meeting, so I suggest he be asked to leave it.' (You could never tell with Bill whether he was making a joke.)

The discussion went on for an hour. The general verdict was that a proper rest should have been given, but that everyone was now prepared to follow the new orders with enthusiasm.

'Before we finish,' said Birch, 'I want to say that this meeting certainly ought never to have been held. Jeans has just said he will communicate to the Germans that the English Group thinks we ought to have a rest. I think you've got no right whatsoever to do that. . . .'

This caused another row. Babs shouted: 'Well, of all the bloody ways to talk about a man. . . . Jeans only does his best and he's got his work cut out already, having to translate as well as give the orders. Why, I've seen the way that man behaved at the front; he's a blooming genius, he's worth ten of you, I can tell you. . . .'

Long after the meeting, Babs went on muttering in this style. 'Jeans is a damned fine communist.'

'Birch is that, too,' I said to him. 'It's only that he was against the whole idea of the meeting.'

Birch was amazed himself at the outburst. He told me he thought Jeans was being a bit difficult, in not translating everything. I rather agreed. Not unnaturally, he objected to having to give everyone's complaint in German, when he himself didn't agree with it. Chris was the only other person who could speak German, but not fluently. I had stood with him at the window, throwing cigarettes and pomegranates to little boys outside. The best way to eat a pomegranate is to suck all the juice out and spit out the rest. Chris had caught a bad chill and looked dejected. I liked him more. He told me a shell had burst a few feet behind him when he was carrying ammunition the first night of the attack.

I found Keith's haversack and extracted two pairs of deliciously warm underclothes. The anarchists had issued them to him in Barcelona. Keith, Norman, Donovan – I hardly thought of them at all. They had just gone, that was all. In the morning there had been a heated discussion about the action, and we all stood up to listen and take part; but every time Jeans or Chris began to translate a few sentences, there would be a loud 'Sh – sh', to allow another German to step forward and say what he thought. One said it was disgraceful that there had been no stretcher-bearers, another that the whole disciplinary system must be changed; someone announced that on the second night a whole company had turned back because of a rumour that Moorish cavalry was approaching. It turned out that about fifteen of the Flems had said they wanted to go home. We left them at Chinchon afterwards and they were sent back to Belgium. Max and Van Renn both said the English Group had had a nasty position the first day and had done very well. I felt rather ashamed as I knew the worst time had been when Bill and I were wandering about lost. Jeans and Birch and Chris and Ray were the people who deserved the praise.

In our group Jerry was more prominent now. He was the best wisecracker. Jock never had anything more original than his familiar dirty song. Joe shouted the loudest, but he was more a master of rhetoric in the form of lavish metaphors in conveying his feelings. He might shout, 'Come here, Jock, you great underdone steak, you fat — , you're a bleeding lame carthorse, you half-cocked bum,' while Jock was limited to ordinary obscenities. Messer had less profusion of language, but was very often in a state of indignation which he expressed with short clipped phrases invoking the Holy Ghost or other deities. He and Jerry shared a 'bed' at Chinchon, and he found a lot to comment on in some of Jerry's bed-time habits.

'Why, you're so crooked, you can't even lie in bed straight,' said Jerry. It was his accent which made this remark a triumph. Jerry and Messer were good friends. One considered them as a unit together, just like Tich and Babs, though they were the more firmly united, because they had come out together and both were ex-soldiers. I was mostly with Birch, though I was very friendly with Bill and Messer and Aussie. Aussie liked doing things by himself. Joe and Jock one considered together, though you could never be sure what Joe was going to do. Everyone liked Ray; or rather, to show how really popular he was, no one disliked him.

We got into Madrid while an air-raid was going on, and saw two planes brought down. We went through the suburbs and were billeted at the little village of Fuencarral, a few miles north. Madrid didn't look very exciting – mostly tram-lines and barricades. They had made it look like a part of London where the road is up and street mending is going on in a lot of places, with braziers heating the workmen's meals. It was an anti-climax.

Our first night in our new quarters we were woken up at one o'clock in the morning, and loaded into lorries. After a cramped and tiring drive, it turned out we had been taken to the wrong front. We went back and there was a row about whether everyone should have the same position as before to make his 'bed'. There wasn't enough room for everyone to be comfortable.

Messer went in to see a dentist the next morning. He told us he was there while there was a big air-raid, and a tram was hit and everyone inside it killed or wounded.

We had to wait a long time for rations; when they arrived they consisted of two raw eggs per person, and bread. Chris had got an acetylene cooker, so we had them all boiled. He was really ill by now and stayed behind. In Fuencarral Aussie and I bought some wine – delicious and sweet like grape juice. That left me six pesetas; I had dropped about eleven through a hole in my pocket. I bought three cigars for a peseta each. Seeing us walking about the street, the villagers whispered to each other: 'They're Russians.'

'What's that, Comrade,' shouted Joe. 'We're English, you know, Ingleses. . . . Rule Britannia – God Save the King – Ingleses!'

'Shut your mouth, you silly fool. You're not in the Luton Town Girl Guides,' from Messer.

In the afternoon we went to occupy a reserve position. We were in a valley surrounded by high ridges. Jeans told us he thought we should be there at least eight days. He told us that the fascists were in the University, that they were prac-tically surrounded and cut off; that the plan was to do nothing for the moment so as to give them a chance to surrender, or attempt to withdraw. Meanwhile we would be able, at last, to do a little 'training'. Bill and Messer and I made a 'bed' together behind a tree, but we were on sloping ground and it was very uncomfortable.

'I don't like this place at all,' said Bill. 'You might well get stray bullets coming this way.'

'Why, there's no danger,' I said.

'Ay,' replied Bill, 'you two are all right; you've got good protection behind me.'

'The man's crazy,' from Messer.

We were half a mile in front of six heavy guns. Each explosion made me start; it was like someone slamming a book just in front of one's nose. Birch suggested we should dig a latrine, then he suggested we should have a political discussion the next day. We did neither. Incidentally, this was the only mention of a latrine that I remember throughout the war. The absence didn't matter at first: but if we were in the same position for a few days, all the ground behind would be covered with mementos. Nearly everybody had diarrhoea at one time or another, which made it worse. Fortunately we were rarely in the same position for more than two or three days.

The first day was warm, and I enjoyed a pleasant sunbath with a cigar and a paper-covered novel. But the eight days' waiting never materialized. The first day was our last. On the second evening, we could hear a continuous racket of machine-gun and rifle fire ahead of us. The rebels were launching an attack in the University City; the artillery barrage started about seven in the evening, shells hurtled over us from both sides, our own guns firing about one for every four of the enemy. About midnight, there was a lull.

We had been crouching in the valley, now the order came to move forward. We went down a road in single file, ten yards between each man, while bullets whistled through the trees overhead. We rested a few hours at a disused pumping station. Just after dawn four battalions of the International Brigade and two Spanish companies launched a counter attack from the north on the rebels.

During the wait before dawn, in the pumping station, Jeans translated some instructions and advice received from the High Command. It was all rather muddled. I remember there was a section about how to meet tanks. Jeans said: 'If the tank is attacking a building you are in, don't run out. A lot of people were killed yesterday by doing this. There is a new method of dealing with tanks now, by lighted petrol bottles. You have the bottle of petrol about half full, then all you have to do is to throw it under the tank.' (This theme, about petrol bottles and tanks, kept on recurring on later occasions; but the advice was wasted as we never saw any petrol bottles and very rarely any matches either.) Another section of the 'advice' struck me as a little odd. It appeared we were to burden ourselves up with spades and picks to strengthen the morale of the Spanish troops. But possibly this was a mistake in the translation.

'Well, now we've finished that,' went on Jeans, 'I have some news I will read. This is an International News Bulletin of the Thaelmann Battalion.' The news he read was sensational. Germany and Italy had recognized General Franco's government, on the pretext that it was in control of Madrid.* Portugal had followed suit. It was suggested that our fight now would have a decisive effect on the future of international relations.

At five o'clock we were waiting, crouched in a ditch at the side of the road. There was a thin drizzle. It did not damp our spirits though. I was excited, and I think most of the others were, too. I found my rifle had jammed, but again Tich was there to mend it. Our immediate objective was a fortress near the Casa Velasquez – three-quarters of a mile from the University of Madrid.

Tich was told to take six men forward to reconnoitre. We ran forward a few yards at a time, then lay flat on the ground, rifles ready with the safety-catch off: Joe was behind Tich, then Babs, Ray and myself, with Messer at the end. It was strangely quiet as the sound of machine-guns sounded far

* This was on 18 November, 1936.

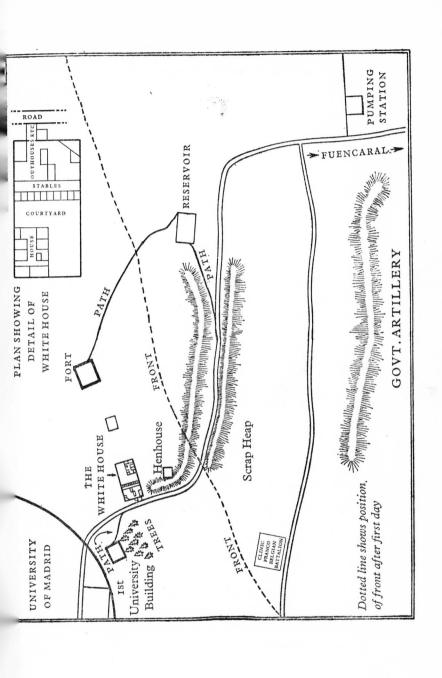

PLAN SHOWING DETAIL OF WHITE HOUSE

ROAD

OUTHOUSES ETC

STABLES

COURTYARD

HOUSE

UNIVERSITY OF MADRID

THE WHITE HOUSE

1st University Building

PATH

TREES

Henhouse

FRONT

FORT

PATH

RESERVOIR

PATH

FRONT

Scrap Heap

CLINIC FRANCO BELGIAN BATTALION

FUENCARAL

PUMPING STATION

GOVT. ARTILLERY

Dotted line shows position of front after first day

away in the distance. Now we were sprinting fast through a wooded valley, I noticed the glistening dew. Just ahead of us was a rectangular reservoir about eighty yards long and fifty yards wide. A few bullets skimmed over it, and we lay down at the side. On the other side a ridge protected us from fire.

'Where the devil does the man think he's taking us to,' muttered Messer. 'He's crazy, this whole outfit's crazy, you can't go walking and trespassing like this.'

In another few minutes, we were behind the wall of the fort. We waited, breathless. There was not a sound from within. The other party of eight Germans under Alex got there at the same time. Alex walked in, then signalled two men to follow him. We waited behind the rampart on the other side.

No one said a word, while Alex battered down a door with the butt of his rifle; then led the way inside, with bayonet fixed. Rifles, mostly caked with mud – ammunition belts, blood-stained caps and other signs of recent occupation lay everywhere. Inside, Alex found heaped together the bodies of twenty Spanish government soldiers. The shell and bullet-hole marks showed the intensity of the rebels' attack. I cleaned the mud off my rifle.

I do not know how long we waited there; first one smack, then another; plaster fell from the walls as machine-gun bullets hit it. The fire was from our right, on the side of the reservoir; the bullets all struck very high and we were well protected. The next thing was a series of heavy crashes. We saw the smoke from shell-bursts a hundred yards away, then a direct hit. Bricks, stones and earth buried four men; no one was badly hurt. A battery of three of our own guns had begun a steady bombardment of the fort. Alex gave the order to retire.

Retiring was not so easy. A few hundred yards from the fort, Alex posted two men behind a tree commanding the path. From their position they could see the fort, and to the right they looked down on the reservoir. The trouble started as we ran back on the side of the reservoir. A brisk fire from short range was opened on us from the other side. The bullets came faster and spat harder into the earth than any we had known before.

'Quick, quicker!' shouted Alex. He and the two Germans behind him had got to the valley where the rising ground sheltered them. As we waited on our stomachs, we heard them opening fire on the enemy. Then I could plainly hear the rat-tat-tat of one – two – three – four separate machine-guns; and they seemed to be from our side. I realized that the whole battalion must have moved up close behind us.

'You O.K., Romilly?' It was Ray, a few yards ahead of me. 'Pass it on to keep absolutely still and wait further orders.'

'O.K., Messer?' I called. There was no reply.

A real battle had started, and it seemed as though we were in the middle. Bullets skimmed across the pond, sometimes sending up a splash of water as they dropped low from their objective. Then we heard shots behind us and a couple of bullets sped over our heads towards the enemy.

'Don't shoot!' shouted someone. 'That's those people that were posted up there.' I was detailed to crawl towards them and tell them what was happening and bring them back. It was a horrid journey. It was soon obvious I could be seen, and I had to go all the way on my stomach. I saw Messer kneeling over the body of a German. Another rolled in a heap a few yards farther on – I only needed one look to see that he was dead.

'God knows if we'll ever get this chap back, or ourselves,' said Messer. 'D'you know those fascists got into that fort a few minutes after we left? For God's sake keep still, man, they'll see you from there!'

It may have been ten minutes or an hour that we waited. It was now quite light. In the valley below the wang-crash of trench mortars' explosions was added to the racket of rifle and machine-guns. An occasional peep showed signs of movement in the fort. Then the battle died down as suddenly as it had begun. We crawled back, dragging the wounded man with us.

By twelve o'clock that morning the Thaelmann Battalion had beaten back the rebels' attack near the reservoir, and, with the Garibaldi Battalion attempted to capture the fort. But on the right, the other side of the Fuencarral road, the fascists advanced, and actually cut the road near the pumping station. The reserve lines on the ridges behind us then came into action, and they had to retire, leaving many dead on the road itself. That night a party of fourteen Moors surrendered at the pumping station.

By evening the fort and the houses to the left could be seen blazing for miles around. Part of the Garibaldi Battalion attempted a bayonet charge and were repulsed. We spent the afternoon on the road as a reserve line.

Two lorries came up with hot soup and coffee. 'Have you heard, boys,' said Ray, 'there's a special rum ration coming along later, and we're going to have thermoses for the coffee?' We spent the night on the road. It was rather miserable as it was impossible to dig oneself in properly at the side, anyway, one was too tired. Most of our blankets were soaked. Messer and I decided to stay up most of the night, so Jeans told us to change the guard. There were three men on duty at a time. One had to keep contact with the Spanish battalion on our right – they had entrenched themselves on the track that went down towards the pond. The other two had to patrol the road on the left. A few hundred yards from where we were, it bent sharply to the right.

At the corner, we paused at the side of the road and gazed forward. The blaze in the night seemed barely fifty yards away. 'Come on,' I said, 'let's see what on earth this is.' We crept forward until we could make out the outlines of the burning houses. If there was anybody there, they did not see us.

When it was Bill's turn, he said: 'My kidneys are something cruel; can you get someone else to do my guard?' The next day Bill went back to the hospital in Fuencarral. I was sorry. Bill was very ill and I did not see him again.

Once I had asked him what he thought of the war, and how it compared with Ireland. 'There's no comparison, I can tell you straight,' he said. 'This is a proper war all right. In Oireland, it would be just a single job as it might be – holding up a transport somewhere, or a surprise attack on a barracks to get prisoners released. It was always an inside job, too, someone – English Tommy it might be, who wanted to make a spot – would open the door or something. And afterwards you'd go home to your fire, and they couldn't get anything on yer – all the lads were in it, you see.'

Later on, I heard that Bill Scott had joined a Spanish battalion and had fought with it for several months before returning to Ireland.

Next morning we attacked the fort and farm buildings. We stood ready in the valley between the road and the ridge ahead of us. Four tanks moved up the road. Rebel artillery was active all the time and occasionally the shells sent up great clouds of smoke near the road; but the tanks chugged slowly on. We watched them out of sight round the bend. Then the poum-poum-poum of their guns showed the attack was in full swing.

The suspense was maddening. I remembered reading books about the War, and for the first time the expression 'going over the top' had some meaning. I felt an urgent desire to relieve myself, but decided there would not be time. Jeans shouted, 'Fix bayonets, everyone ready!' The Italians were lying ready on the ridge. They would cover us with rifle fire. Behind the road, four machine-guns started up.

'Forward! Rush ten yards, drop, wait for next advance, everyone to fire at the windows,' shouted Jeans.

We reached the wall of the White House. It was a mad scramble. We kept near the road, and the bullets skimmed over harmlessly at first. Then there was a space of fifty yards, running all out, in threes. A few of the Germans dropped on the way – it was just like seeing people killed running in an American film.

All the English got there safely. Most of the fire came from the red house. Outside the wall were the bodies of Moorish soldiers – some still groaning. Machine-guns from the Clinic Hospital were taking a deadly toll of the defenders. No one could escape by the road behind.

We entered a courtyard. It was like a large farm, with a series of barns, workshops and armouries in separate apartments on either side. A deadly machine-gun fire from the second shed on our left made us stop; a party under Alex was storming the National Guard building on the right. A German pulled a Mills bomb from his pocket, extracted the pin with his teeth; he stood up, bullets whistling past him, and hurled it in. We rushed in after its explosion. Four Moors had been firing from behind a dead horse. Now they were finished. A shell crashed into the next shed. Peering cautiously through the window, we saw one of our tanks had come right up outside. It was firing alternately at the stables and at a little house on the other side of the road. A man got out, and waved his arm at us. We could not tell what he meant, but waited in the barn with the dead Moors and the horse; a tremendous crash made the wall on our right crumble in debris.

'Look out!' shouted Birch, dragging me with him to the floor. A figure had lunged through an opening in the mass of bricks and wood which separated us from the next-door shed. The man was dead; his body hung suspended over the debris, making a barrier between the two apartments, his head tilted slowly forward and his red cap slipped on to the ground.

We reached the wall at the end after clambering through eight more separate sheds. In that farm the Moors left at least a hundred dead. Most were not killed by bullets – their bodies had been torn apart by shells, limbs blown off by hand grenades. The farm was fifty yards wide. Two mangy cows wandered aimlessly about. They were wounded, but their hides seemed too tough for the bullets. In the middle of the mud I watched a little blaze crackling away – two dead men were burning steadily.

103

Joe and Babs were in the little house across the road. It was once the residence of the commander of the National Guard. There were signs of a meal – curtains, a bed, an armchair – but everything was smashed up. There was no one in the house. Joe and Babs paused a moment to look at their faces in a mirror hanging on the wall – a second later the glass splintered and fell as bullets struck it.

We could see Moors running down the road towards the University. We opened fire. Everyone was a little drunk at the sight of the enemy in open retreat. I fired wildly, never stopping to take aim, I was desperate to discharge as many shots as I could now – for the first time in the war – I had a clear target.

We captured the stables and the guard house. The fort and the little red house just by it were still held by the fascists. One of our tanks had been destroyed on the road by a direct hit from a fascist shell. Early in the afternoon the enemy rallied his forces, and we were isolated between the fort on the one side and the first buildings of the University on the other. Machine-gun fire from both sides made any move seem impossible. It was not safe even to cross from one side of the farm to the other without going right back and round the wall. The two little houses on the other side of the road we evacuated almost as soon as we had occupied them. Whichever way we attacked we would be under cross fire. No reinforcements in any number could come up because the road was under fire. The path from the hen-house to the farm was our only means of communication, and this – for twenty yards – brought us under the machine-guns of the fort.

We waited in the hen-house. 'May as well kill some of these birds and have a good feed, anyway,' said Joe. 'Probably poisoned,' said somebody, and that thought was enough to make us leave them.

Later Max asked for volunteers. Birch and Ray and Messer and Tich and Ovenden and myself and three Germans altogether were given spades. We waited behind the wall of

104

the White House, a few yards from the road on our left. 'Everyone, in turn, to run out and dig in behind a tree,' said Max. We had to make a line of dug-outs to the left of the farm, facing the University building.

Hans ran out first and flopped down behind a tree ten yards the other side of the road; Tich went next; we thought they had got him when he dropped at the same place, but then he got up and scrambled on to a tree farther away; Karl was next, but they hit him as he started to cross the road – a bullet straight through his forehead. Someone got his body; it left a red smear on the road. I felt a little sick. The enemy had some first-class marksmen, and a lot of men who moved a few feet out of safety got a bullet through their heads that afternoon. Messer and Ray arrived all right; Ray had a long way to run. I realized I should have ten yards farther. The spade was heavy and cumbersome; after sprinting across the road, I lumbered and lurched the rest of the way.

It was worse when I had got to my tree. The bullets went everywhere – through the branches above, whistled straight past my head and the tree in front on either side, threw up the earth around or thudded into the bark. The spade was too heavy. I could not use it without raising myself up. I tore up the earth with my hands, and cursed when I bruised them on the roots of the tree. A caking of mud got into my nose and eyes and teeth. In five minutes it was better – I had thrown up a little barrier of earth for protection. Someone else had run out – Schiemann, the German in charge of the party – so I was not the farthest of all from safety.

'Take orders from the left,' Ray shouted.

'Get them in English as well as German,' I replied.

Soon we got the order to fire at the windows of the houses opposite. They seemed near. My rifle was practically buried in the mud. We picked off a few of the enemy who were outside the protection of their wall. Whatever our job might be, I didn't think seven men with rifles, with a few handfuls of earth for protection, could do much. Then they started using trench mortars. I gave up firing and waited, still on the ground, listening to the crash of the enemy's rifles and the rat-tat of their machine-guns as they swept us with fire. The first bomb fell between me and the German on the left. It was like being shelled by artillery only you heard the whiz-z-z much louder.

'Back! Back!' shouted Schiemann; he ran back behind me. Later he was taken back to hospital with shell-shock; I stayed there and thought everything out clearly; mentally I scored off various points on my fingers: first, I did not want to be killed; secondly, I did not think I should be. I thought a bullet would hit me in the arm or shoulder, my arm would be numbed completely and there wouldn't be much pain; I should wake up in a bed in a hospital and there wouldn't be any bombs or shells or aeroplanes or tanks or bullets in sight or sound. But there was a snag – one would not ever get back; I decided it would be best if the bullet never got me at all.

Max gave the order to return one by one: 'Remember to get the mud off your boots,' shouted Ray. I hoped it would be a long time before my turn came. The others made their journeys in stages, flopping down behind a tree every ten yards. I decided to run straight on, waiting would be awful. I didn't bother about the spade. A few yards from the road I missed my footing on the slippery ground, and fell head first. I heard Joe say: 'Looks as if he got one.' I thought so myself at first, but I had fallen into a large shell-hole.

'Where's my rifle?' I shouted. I groped out with my arm and got it. The shell-hole gave far more protection than my tree. I felt quite confident, and fired off five rounds.

'Good shot, that's the way, boy,' said Joe. They were all standing with Max and Alex behind the wall of the farm. I had hardly taken any aim, but apparently one of my shots had got a fascist carrying ammunition. A few seconds later I thought my ear-drum was broken – a deafening explosion seemed right on top. This must be another trench mortar.

106

But it was one of our tanks which had come right up behind me.

Max shook hands with us and congratulated us. We cleaned our rifles with oil in the front room of the National Guard building. There were dead lying in the room, in the passage, and heaped up on the stairs. No one bothered to move them. A machine-gun post was established behind a window on the first floor to command the little red house and the fort. Every ten minutes someone would be carried down wounded from that window.

'Five fascist tanks are on the way, boys,' said Jock. The rumour was passed around. Our own tanks – all except two – had gone back.

'You're a damn fool,' said Birch, 'passing round a silly tale like that. What sort sort of good do you think that's going to do?'

'If you ask me, we've done about enough today,' said Messer, and Jerry, 'You'll have done enough when some Moor sticks his bayonet up your arse, and then you'll get the V.C. When I came out here, they told me this was a revolution, but it's nothing but a — war.'

Jeans came in. 'They want three volunteers to form an anti-squad with hand grenades.'

Birch said 'O.K.'; nobody else said anything. Fortunately the order was changed, and there weren't any enemy tanks. We munched a few bits of bread that one or two men had brought in their ammunition belts. This day seemed to have lasted very long already. I couldn't remember any further back than the pumping station, and that was yesterday morning. I hoped it would get dark soon. I did not want any more fighting today.

We talked about 'morale'. I said I thought hot food was the most important point. They brought some soup up in a lorry at five o'clock when it was getting dark. We ate it outside the house in a steady drizzle. We were all grouped together. No one was doing any firing now.

'If they made an attack now,' whispered Babs to Tich,

'we'd be fairly finished. Jesus Christ, is this all there is left of this bunch?'

They were forming up the groups and zugs and companies. The 1st Company was barely sixty strong; Paul was wounded, and Arnold was now leader of the complete 3rd Zug, and Tich of our group, which was the only one in any company that had suffered no casualties. As usual, the machine-gunners had lost most. The rain was heavier now, but it had no effect on the steadily burning fires. I was surprised that the walls and doors did not fall in – but each little bit of the building was burning separately. Nobody took any notice of them. The burning, with the overpowering stench inside the house, gave an atmosphere of unhealthiness and decadence; I do not know of any word to describe that peculiar combination of dead men, crackling flames and drizzle.

We carried back some of our own dead on stretchers, and parties of men worked to give them a common grave. The farm and the National Guard building were evacuated and we were back again in our old position on the road that night.

Jeans told us the next morning that the High Command (whatever and wherever that might be) was very pleased with the English Group.

Chapter 8

Tich said he thought we were sure to be reinforced on the next day. He was wrong. We spent five more days entrenched on the road, in the course of which time we were bombed, shelled, machine-gunned from the air, practically frozen, visited by an English journalist, and instructed in the use of trench mortars. Other achievements included building of dug-outs and learning how these should not be built and where they should not be built; and holding our positions during an attack which lasted from six in the morning till five in the afternoon.

It was my first experience of digging. I did not like it. In fact, I can imagine few things more disagreeable. Hacking away with a pick is not so bad – the disagreeable part is shovelling up the earth with a spade. As originally planned, there should have been one dug-out for two men at the least. As it was, laziness and general dislike of digging resulted in no more than two proper dug-outs altogether. Both were far too small. My companions were Joe and Jock and Sid and Birch and Jerry. Joe found a piece of corrugated iron which we stuck over the top of ours. It made a comfortable shed – for two people. Even Jock's experience with the Territorial Army never prompted him to suggest we should make any arrangements for firing through the parapet. An order was given for men to sleep with ammunition belts fastened round them.

'Don't know what we're going to do about Jerry,' said Joe. 'Can't say the little bastard hasn't worked; we'll have to take it in turns for one man to sleep outside, that's all.'

As we were all on duty at different times, one hardly ever got more than an hour's consecutive sleep.

At the corner of the road, where it bent round towards the White House, we established an observation post. To get to it you had to run a hundred yards – very often under fire. The best thing was to wait till a bullet came whistling down the road, then make a dash all out. Direct communication with the hospital building was impossible. At one point we were all certain it was occupied by the enemy. No one ever knew for sure who was in it. 'Better call them guys neutrals,' said Jerry.

In two days' time, and after a brisk skirmish between a German and Italian patrol in the valley, we did at least know that the ridge immediately ahead was occupied by an Italian company. This meant that in one sense we were a reserve line. On the other hand, so far as anything coming down the road was concerned, we were a front line position.

The Italians kept up a constant fire all day and night. This was annoying for us, as the enemy always replied and a regular strafing went on over us. I agreed with Messer when he said it was most unfair we should get the bullets meant for the Italians. We never managed a satisfactory password.

After the skirmish referred to above a party of Germans brought back five 'prisoners' in triumph and announced that their men had surrounded an enemy patrol. It was our own front line position they had practically surrounded, and their prisoners were men of the Garibaldi Battalion. The Germans were very disappointed. The Italian leader told the interpreter that the next time his trench was sprayed with bullets by the Germans they would return the compliment. Relations got better after that, and we placated the Italians by taking up extra rum rations for them at night.

The dug-outs on our right, stretching down towards the pond, were far more elaborate than ours. They looked like a row of Red Indian huts (not that I have ever seen a row of Red Indian huts, but this is what I imagined they look like). We tried to copy them, without much success.

110

Sometimes for an hour on end, the whole front was silent. One could stroll in safety on the road behind. One morning three officers came up to inspect the position – Alex,* Willie and Beimler (the political commandant). Willie had the same reputation as Alex for reckless courage; he had led the attack in the Guard House while we had been fighting in the stables, and had thrown hand grenades into every room on the first floor; he was the sort of man who would walk in front of a tank to encourage its driver in the attack.

We heard his bullet. Everyone heard its whine for several seconds – it was the sort experts called 'spent bullet' – the little group on the road heard it, stopped and glanced in the direction of the sound. We heard it all the way and we heard it reach its mark as Willie clutched his stomach and stumbled on to the ground. Much later we heard his lung was hit. Willie's part in the war was finished. He died in a hospital in Barcelona.

It was the day before the attack that Jeans told us an English journalist had come up to see us. 'There is a man from the *Paris-soir*, and someone from an English paper; he may be a fascist, you should be careful what you say,' he told us.

At first everyone was reticent, but after five minutes we were all prepared to excuse Sefton Delmer for the politics of the *Daily Express*; and we all wanted to hear the news from England.† 'What was there on the front page of the *Express* before you left?' I asked.

He told us his editor had hesitated to send him the week before as it seemed certain Madrid would fall. His remark that we were occupying the most vital sector of the Madrid defence was received with mixed feelings. Joe was entirely in his element.

'I used to learn soldiering watching the Terriers on a Sun-

* Alex Maass, a popular star of Cologne Radio before Hitler.

† Sefton Delmer (born 1904) was then a prominent foreign reporter on the *Express*. He had previously been in Germany. His meeting with Romilly is mentioned in his book, *Trail Sinister*.

day afternoon,' he told the journalist. 'We've got nothing to complain of here except the Russian grub and the Fritzies now and again.'

Birch gave him a scowl, but it didn't worry Joe, and he went on: 'Yes, you can tell 'em in Luton – that's where I come from, you know – that I'm going to march down the High Street with my medals, and I hope the Public Assistance Officer's there to see me.'

'I think you all know Keith Scott Watson,' said Delmer.

He told us Keith was working with him in Madrid. I asked him to give him my good wishes and tell him I would come and look him up if ever we got leave. Delmer asked us if there was anything we particularly wanted, and promised before he went to get us newspapers and chocolate and cigarettes.

When he had gone, Joe was put properly in the dock for the way he had been talking. Birch was chief prosecutor, but I was surprised to see Messer was also thoroughly sick with him. I thought they made a stupid fuss about it.

There were several alarms that night, when we all stood ready, knocking each other over in the narrow trench. The observation post was under continual fire. At about eight o'clock, Joe and I were on duty there together. Every two minutes one of us would pop our head over the top to have a look round between the bullets.

'What's that?' I said. 'Doesn't that look like someone?'

Joe peered over, then shouted into the night: 'Here you, there, Alto! Come on, Alto!'

He shot back the safety catch and pressed the butt of his rifle against his shoulder.

'Wait a minute,' I whispered, 'it may be one of our men.'

'Shoot first; ask questions afterwards, that's the way, boy,' said Joe.

His shot started the whole line into action. Ten minutes later we heard someone shouting: 'Englishmen, come back.'

It was Messer trying to tell us that it was time to change the guard. But the words caused a minor panic on the road;

and for another hour men were anxiously challenging each other and muttering 'fascisti', 'faschisten', 'fascists'.

Just before dawn an aeroplane circled slowly twice over us, and dropped a load of bombs on the road between our positions and the White House. We watched it return and saw its light go down behind the enemy's lines – it seemed barely half a mile away, beyond the fort, that it landed. We thought the rebels would not make a direct attack on our position for reasons of military strategy – they would try and force our men to evacuate the hospital building, and at the same time press forward on our right where the ground was more favourable.

Soon after the aeroplane's visit, they started shelling the hospital. One of the shells hit the road, but some fell unpleasantly near us. The observation post had been evacuated ten minutes before a six-inch shell enlarged it. It was our first real experience of shelling – I can only compare it to the sensation of being in a very rough sea, waiting for each new wave to burst, hoping you may get beyond it or in front of it. It kept us three hours in our dug-outs and the food lorry never came up the road that morning. Eighteen Junkers came over us later and bombed our artillery positions. After that the heavy guns behind us were silent for a while.

All this time I had the pleasant illusion that the bombing and shelling did not actively concern us. I somehow could never really believe the enemy were occupying themselves with *us*; we were only playing at soldiers, we were only amateurs. It seemed impossible that over there, beyond the outline of the fort, someone was scheming how *we* were to be destroyed, eliminated, or – the simplest and most expressive word of all – just killed. Delmer had said we were holding the most vital position; it was ridiculous that we should be doing this – who were surely concerned all the time only with seeing that we had the same food rations as the Flems and quarrelling among ourselves and holding Group Meetings. It was all wrong.

I thought about all this as we stood waiting, sometimes

gazing over the parapet at the Italians ahead on the ridge, waiting for the attack. The next thing that happened that morning was over almost before we realized it. We thought nothing of the familiar words: *'Fliege, Decke!'* – as they were shouted down the line, until the three gigantic birds had swept right over us spraying machine-gun bullets into the valley below, and I saw someone raise his rifle to his shoulder as though to shoot, and then they were gone as swiftly as they had come. By great good luck, not one man was hit, as all the bullets from the aeroplanes went into the valley between the Thaelmann and Garibaldi lines.

The order was given for a general move down the road to the right, so that we should not be surprised by a tank attack from the White House. We moved into better dug-outs where the Germans had made proper firing positions. Jeans hurried from one to the other, seeing everyone was well placed, and shepherding Sid, who had found nowhere to go. I made a firing step with my haversack and an empty ammunition box. Then I sat down and read my book about snobbery in the United States of America. The shelling was dying down now, but there was an increasing racket of rifle and machine-gun fire. A man who required to relieve himself was forced to do so in his own dug-out, as the road behind was under fire.

The tempo of the firing grew and I abandoned my book and sat with my rifle on my knees. I wondered what the time was. There was a lull in the battle just before we heard the first rumours, whispered from mouth to mouth – 'Spanish troops on our right are in full retreat.'

We were in a bad position. It was impossible to move more than a quarter of a mile down the road – to retreat to the ridge behind brought us under direct fire of the White House and the fort. We knew nothing of what was happening. Jeans had gone to find out. We could only remain – and wait. I felt frightened.

The firing started again – now it was much louder and nearer – one was more conscious of the bullets. They thudded into the bank below our barricades. The Garibaldi men came back – some wounded, some dragging machine-guns. Singly and in groups we saw them descend the slope into the valley. Volunteers scrambled down the bank with stretchers and brought some of the wounded. There was nothing to be done with them; they could only be left in the trenches. To have attempted to get them back by the road would have been madness; some were left in the open.

All I got was a blurred picture from occasional quick glances over the top; then, with the last mad scramble of men as the Italians joined us on the road, we knew the front line was evacuated. They had held it against bombs, trench mortars, and a continual machine-gun fire from close range. Then the fire had come from the right, infiltrating their narrow trench. It made evacuation and *sauve qui peut* the only policy. They crowded into our dug-outs. There was no panic, no sign of disorderly retreat. Now that the danger was definite, now rumour was fact, now the attack was a reality, everyone was calm. There was even an exaggerated calmness in the passing on of orders, in remarks about how we should all stand to or the amount of ammunition we possessed.

Jeans came back – and about forty men were grouped behind him. The sloping ground to the right was difficult to hold. It was all quite plain now – we were going to make a stand on that four hundred yard stretch of level road.

'Keep your heads down,' said Jeans. 'No one is to fire till the order is given. There are four machine-guns behind us. If an enemy tank comes down, no one is to move while the anti-tank squad deals with it.'

In answer to breathless questions, he told us: 'Our line has been broken half a mile down, but our machine-guns are still commanding the road. Sixteen Russian tanks are on the way' (cheers from everyone, 'About time them fellows showed up, heard enough about them,' from Joe); 'if we have to retire to the other road behind we shall be protected by them.'

There were about two hundred of us, all bunched close together. Perhaps half an hour elapsed – perhaps more; it started with two men falling dead from close-range bullets in a dug-out near by. Then the real hailstorm of lead came at us. I was lying flat on my stomach. We shoved in clip after clip of cartridges until the breaches and barrels of our guns were red hot. I never took aim. I never looked up to see what I was firing at. I never heard the order to open fire. I never saw the enemy – never knew for certain where they were – these things were talked over afterwards. My head was in a whirl – I was almost drunk with the smell of powder. I remember a young Spaniard next to me, wondering what he was doing and how he got there; but there was no time to work it all out. It was a mad scramble – pressing my elbows into the earth, bruising them on the stones, to get my rifle to my shoulder, pressing the trigger, rasping back the bolt, then shoving it home, then on to my elbows again.

We never learned how long it had all been – how long before Alex shouted 'Forward,' and stumbled down the bank first, waving a muddy bayonet in his hand. Jock and Birch and Messer never stopped talking for days afterwards about the Moors they'd picked up – I was not on that job – and they all had an odd assortment of knives and scarves and boots.

'Ah was goin' to have his beard and dress meself like a Moor to give ye all a fright,' Jock told us, 'only Alex woudna let me, he said you boys'd all be on the run at the first sight of that beard.'

I foresaw there would be calls on volunteers to dig a grave for the Moors, so I busied myself with other jobs. Ray and I went round collecting ammunition – and later on we went to the ridge ahead and returned in triumph with three boxes we had found hidden in one of the dug-outs. When the lorry brought us up hot soup and meat, and tins of chicken and eggs and cheese and coffee with milk that night, we were too tired, too excited to eat and sleep. We just wanted to talk about it all.

The fascist attack had failed. The Moors had never crossed the road. The presence of the Russian tanks may have been a deterrent (we never saw or heard anything more of these and more than one sceptic among us cast doubts upon their existence); but at any rate, at no point could they cross the road. In several places they reached the Government lines on the other side of the reservoir, then attempted a direct attack on our positions to clear the way for an advance down the road, and at the same time surround the hospital building. They had occupied the Italians' line (three hundred yards away), but they were never able to get established in their trenches or to attempt to cross the valley. All who scrambled over the parapet had to face a withering fire from our lines. Time and again the accurate range of their marksmen claimed a victim among the machine-gunners behind us; each time we would redouble our fire while someone else slipped back to take the dead man's place.

I have seen accounts of attacks in newspapers which tell you about men, yielding ground 'inch for inch', and everything sounds romantic and spectacular. It may seem like that afterwards. At the time all is blurred and confused. You do not know what is happening – probably your one thought is to keep your head down.

Chapter 9

Early the next morning we occupied the White House and the stables. There was no resistance, and any casualties the fascists may have had from the previous action had been removed. Everything was very quiet. Peering cautiously ahead we could see the windows of the University of Madrid; there was no sign of life. Little groups of Germans wandered up and down the road freely. The two little houses were empty and so was the first University building – that house we should remember so well, from whose windows we had been sprayed with bullets lying out behind the trees. All that seemed years ago. Returning to the White House was like going back to school.

We spent a week in the White House – it was a more dangerous position than the road, but I thought this was more than made up for by the greater comfort, for we had mattresses to sleep on, and, most important, we had warmth. The first day and night were eventful. A dozen men were killed and as many wounded in an attempt to capture the fort. It was Alex's scheme. The little red house was deserted. We clustered inside the White House, and two hand grenades were distributed to each man. They were the sort that have to be lit by wicks, then thrown as soon as the wick is sizzling. We were given cigarettes to be able to light the grenades with the burning ash. Joe was sick from smoking.

You were supposed to light the hand grenades, hurl them at the fort, then run forward full speed to the wall at the little red house, and take up position there covering the windows and firing-holes of the fort. We all knew it would fail – at least the English did.

'This is the craziest idea I ever heard,' said Messer. He told Harry the fat Swiss, who commanded the second group, what he thought.

'Of course zey are craazee, zese Germans,' said Harry. 'Zey want to beat their breasts and die.'

I left them and found everyone more or less shared their ideas – we thought the prospects gloomy.

A few minutes later I heard Messer's voice: 'These chaps make me sick. If you don't like this scheme tell him so yourself. Why don't you tell Alex? D'you think I'm going to tell him for you. Of all the gutless bunch I've ever come across. . . .'

Alex went first. He only got ten yards, and Birch and I managed to get his body. There were no stretchers – no ambulance service. I ran back to the hen-house and signalled to the troops in our old positions. No one wanted to come further than the hen-house – I cursed them and ran back to show them there weren't many bullets.

But the worst part began when we got him on the stretcher. There were four of us, Birch and Messer and myself and one of the Red Cross men; we took one pole each. We started slowly and kept our rifles slung over our shoulders so that the enemy from the windows of the fort could make no mistake about what we were doing. The ambulance man wore a Red Cross flag on his arm. It may have been a stray bullet at first, but two seconds later the regular swish-swish-swish made us quicken our pace. The stretcher and its occupant were dropped.

'Go slowly, you fool,' whispered Birch to Messer. 'All right, give me the whole thing then; let the thing alone, man.'

He seized both the poles at the front and advanced steadily. Messer tried to relieve him, but he cursed him to leave the thing alone.

Behind the walls of the hen-house the other ambulance men met us and took Alex back to safety. While I sat down to get my breath back, Birch and Messer argued about how the stretcher should have been carried.

'Well, I'm going back,' said Birch finally. 'We didn't have any instructions for taking a siesta here.'

He returned, not bothering to run or hurry through the danger area. Messer shrugged his shoulders. I agreed with him.

As we had all guessed, the attack failed, and that night the enemy occupied the little red house and barricaded the windows. We settled down to the work of drilling holes in the sheds of the farmyard, and setting up positions behind the windows. There was a ten-yard stretch where only a low barricade of sandbags gave protection. There someone had stuck up a piece of paper with a skull and cross-bones, and written underneath the words: 'Beware of Hitler's bullets.'

All day another section of the Thaelmann Battalion attacked the fort from the other side. Again they failed.

There were fifty of us in the White House that night. Four officers in addition to Alex were killed or wounded, and a young German called Oswald took command. On the extreme left of the wall, we built a barricade right across the road. The stables were never fortified, they and the two houses the other side of the road and the first University building were all No-Man's-Land. From the top windows was an excellent view of the University, and we were able to open fire on everyone we saw approaching or leaving.

On the first night I was part of a group which had the job of patrolling the stables. Harry was in charge. I asked him what we were supposed to be doing, and where the enemy was supposed to be, and what liaison we had.

He said: 'Zere are two ways zee enemy may attack; maybe it weel be tomorrow with tanks and aeroplanes and shells, or perhaps in ze night ze black ones will sneak up. Zat is what you have to watch. If you zee a black one – they can go very quietly – you shoot at once and make a great noise to frighten heem.'

It was a bitter cold night, and I wrapped my blanket close round me, not at all pleased with the prospect of meeting a 'black one'.

Next day all was quiet though we knew the enemy were only a few hundred yards from us. We were now beginning to feel the effects of eight days without proper sleep and rest, and we moved about feeling heavy and sticky and dirty – it was an exaggeration of the sensation you have after driving a car a very long way. We wondered when we should be relieved, and this formed the main topic of our conversation. Inside the house there was still the unpleasant smell of the dead, though these had all been removed and buried. We all agreed we were a ridiculously small force to face an enemy attack, and our spirits were lower than they had been at any time. The casualties among the Germans were enormous – in eight days they had had over a hundred casualties – nearly all the old leaders had disappeared. Our little group almost felt guilty in having miraculously escaped with not a single casualty.

On the second night Tich was in charge of the guard. Our zug was responsible for protecting the right-hand side of the Guard House – at the end of the wall two men lay flat behind a barricade, fifty yards away from the enemy in the little red house, while another man patrolled the valley, behind Birch and Aussie and I were on guard together and we shared a mattress for our rest periods. 'May as well take our boots off, don't you think?' said Aussie as we lay down. 'A man's got to have a rest.'

We laughed. Aussie's withered old face broke into a kindly puzzled smile, with the corners of the lips like those of someone who is being coy, when we remonstrated with this idea. Though he kept his boots on, it took Aussie the best part of ten minutes to get ready when our turn for guard came at last. We had three spells of two hours – from eight till ten, from two till four, and again from seven till nine in the morning.

The hours of sleep were precious. I can't remember any other time in my life when I have so much enjoyed the prospect of sleeping. When you first felt the hand on your shoulder and heard someone saying: 'Your turn on guard now,' you would hope it was a dream and you could go on with a delicious sleep. But when you came back, chattering with cold, you were impatient with others who were like that. Jerry was the worst offender; he was not slow, like Aussie, he just pretended not to wake up.

When we stumbled out into the passage at two o'clock Tich was sitting huddled up like a fat owl, enveloped in his blanket.

'Take a swig of this,' said Aussie, putting a bottle of brandy to his lips.

'Well, don't forget that's got to do for the whole lot of them,' said Tich.

Aussie looked brighter after his drink. 'Half these men don't appreciate the stuff,' he whispered to me. 'Have you got a flask there? Fill it up, man, fill it up.'

At the right-hand corner of the house, where we were supposed to be keeping a watch, we found the barricades were quite ineffective, so I set to work to fill up sacks with earth, and pile them into a proper barrier. I soon got tired of lying with my elbows pressed to the ground, and decided to sit on a chair with the rifle across my knees. Birch argued at first, pointing out how dangerous this might be, but I thought comfort more important.

He was worried about the slack state of everything. 'What the devil's the good of these hand grenades?' he said. 'We haven't got any matches. I asked Tich and he said there weren't any, and I told Jeans. Look at the state we found this barricade in.'

Jeans, when the hand grenade question was explained for the fourth or fifth time, had told Birch not to take things too seriously.

'Look at Aussie now,' he went on, 'he'll be half asleep when he's here on guard. . . . For Christ's sake, look out where you're pointing your rifle.' It turned out his remark about Aussie was well founded.

Every half-hour we changed positions, and a different man out of the three of us would be walking up and down while the other two kept watch. Aussie settled down and made himself comfortable on his stomach. I spoke to him and got no answer. His rifle was pointing limply forward at the ground. He was asleep. We chuckled over this for a long time and, needless to say, we did not inform Birch.

The next incident that night was a few minutes later. Tich hurried up and gave us whispered instructions to open rapid fire straight ahead. We fired ten rounds without any reply from the enemy. Someone had seen two of them sneaking up with hand grenades. We fired another ten rounds. A few bullets struck the wall over our head. I went back to investigate, but on the way met a messenger from the Spanish machine-gunners in the hen-house behind us who had come to apologize for the accidental 'strafing' they had given us.

There was no more firing that night, and on our 'sector' all was quiet. But at the other end of the wall there was more cause for alarm. A Frenchman came up and asked me to interpret a message to the commander. He was very excited, and said they had seen a tank approaching down the road. I told Tich and he went inside to wake up Jeans. I informed him, making it sound as interesting as possible, and copying the Frenchman's expressive shrugs ('*Ah, ça, vous savez, ça c'est formidable; ça, ce n'est pas bon, qu'est ce qu'on peut faire donc?*').

The message came back from the commander: 'It is very unlikely a tank will attack at night. Keep me informed of any future developments.'

A fascist tank came up the road from the University City the next morning. It was fast and looked like a gigantic beetle – it was mounted with machine-guns, and we differentiated it from our own at once by the absence of the long-nosed pom-pom gun. We expected this was the beginning of an attack, but as soon as our machine-guns opened fire, it turned back and vanished out of sight. This incident roused our spirits a lot. It was the last we saw of a fascist tank.

There were rumours of an intended bayonet charge on the fort that day. Birch said to Jeans: 'Put my name down as a volunteer, will you? I don't want to be left out'; and he said to me, 'Are you going to put down your name?'

I said no, I would wait and see what happened and whether they asked for volunteers.

'Heaven knows why they can't bring up a tank and shell that place so that we can get into the first house,' said Birch.

'The ground's too muddy,' said Tich. 'I think those tank drivers don't like the idea of getting stuck out there!'

A Spanish company had come up in the night and occupied the first University building on the other side of the road. After the tank incident, we were a bit more cautious in sauntering across to make their acquaintance, and the only comparatively safe way was to crawl across on your stomach behind the barricades. We could not make out why there was no fire from the fascists in the other University buildings. All that day we saw not a sign of action though the Spaniards continually peppered their windows with bullets.

We were envious of the Spaniards' feeding arrangements. They cooked all the food themselves in big saucepans and served delicious hot meals of liver and bacon. Our stuff was all tinned, a whole day's supply being brought up by lorry at night. 'Of course, I could do the job myself,' said Tich, 'like I did with the Buffs in the Great War, ran a proper field kitchen; come to that, I could do it for the whole company if we wanted it.'

We all agreed, and continually pressed the point with the Germans. That week in the White House, we had ample experience of Tich's cooking and organizing ability – we gave him our rations of raw eggs, raw ham and bread, and he made hot meals with them, and at the same time we had our coffee warmed up. All that week the timber roofs of the buildings went on burning steadily; sometimes a beam would fall, but it made no difference to the even progress of the smouldering.

There was one day of heavy bombardment. '*Fliege, Decke!*' and half an hour watching planes circling overhead gave me an unpleasant feeling that the quiet, inefficient calm of the

124

previous days was going to be interrupted. But when they dropped bombs – a long way back, in the ridges behind us – it looked very neat, like birds making careful little messes from a tree. The first shell was a shock after that. It exploded in a cloud of smoke and earth and sent hot, jagged metal on the road. The machine-gunners behind the barricade scrambled for the shelter of the wall. We all huddled behind, as though by standing with a solid wall between our backs and the enemy, we could be immune.

I was standing next to Babs. 'That's going to get us,' I muttered as the shrieking whistle grew nearer.

'That! That's meant for the supplies and transport if there were any.'

He was right – the shell went well overhead. Three times we heard six-inch shells crash into the stables and the White House, each crash followed a second later by the crumbling noise of destructions, as doors and walls and tables collapsed.

Birch wanted to find out whether they were using shrapnel or high explosive. 'That's high explosive all right,' said Tich. 'If that had been shrapnel, those fellows on that barricade would have known it.'

The bombardment went on sporadically all day. We would grow accustomed to the familiar wang-wang-wang of the artillery duel that was being fought over our heads, then would come the sudden shock of a burst near the house. They scored no more hits though, and the barricade on the road was re-established. We cheered heartily when three of their shells dropped one after another between the fort and the little red house, and the fourth smacked into its walls. We had been told the enemy in the fort were desperate and might withdraw in the night or surrender. The order was given to stand by ready to fire if they attempted to retreat under cover of the bombardment, but under no circumstances to shoot if they came forward to give themselves up.

The sixth day was cloudy. I was glad to say good-bye to the sun: it meant saying good-bye to the fascist aeroplanes as well. Jeans bustled about that morning, seeing that everyone's rifle was cleaned – he was accompanied by three German and Spanish officers, and was evidently anxious to impress them with our efficiency.

Joe straightened himself, his face flushed and beaming. 'Morning, colonel,' he shouted, and clicked his heels in salute. 'Now then, my men, the herm haw General wishes to say a few words haw. . . .'

'Stop playing the fool, Joe,' from someone, 'you make us look like a Sunday School.'

We did the attacking that day. By ten o'clock, a thin misty rain covered the country. The heavy guns were silent as Government troops advanced on the right of the fort. The enemy machine-gunners blazed away as the mist grew thicker, but by midday our men had surrounded the fort – that was the message we received. Jeans took a patrol to investigate the ruins of the little red house. It was empty. At four o'clock the mist lifted slightly, and a white flag hung from a window of the fort. The Italians – part of the Garibaldi Battalion who had surrounded it – rushed forward, calling on the enemy to throw out their arms. At twenty yards range the fascist machine-gunners opened a withering fire.

We learned all this two hours later, crouching behind the windows of the red house, waiting for orders, knowing nothing of what was happening the other side of the fort. An intense fire against the little red house, where we had no proper barricades, made it impossible for us to see what was happening. There were six of us. Each time someone shouted back for instructions, the reply came, 'Keep still!'

When it was dark, we crept back. Ray told us what had happened: 'They're going to get back the bodies of some of those Italians tonight,' he said.

At three in the morning we were relieved. We marched half a mile in single file down the valley, then on to the road, and as far as the tunnel at the cross-roads, where the lorries were waiting. It was light by the time they started up, and the Germans were singing. We had been jammed close together on the journey to the front. Now there were barely half a dozen men in some of the lorries. Near the road, wooden crosses marked the spot where many Germans had been buried. As the lorries rumbled past them, the men stood up to attention, fists clenched:

'*Rot Front.*'

✳

That same day, after we had gone, the enemy launched an attack on the White House. The Uuiversity building was evacuated under a three-hour artillery bombardment. Aeroplanes dropped more than a ton of explosive bombs. Tanks came up the road and the defenders were driven from room to room. When night came the Casa Velasquez had fallen, and once more the stairs were choked with the bodies of the dead. In those little ruined buildings no bigger than an English farm, the death-roll had mounted fast.

Chapter 10

We had a bath at Fuencarral. It consisted of a tub – and cold water; the soap was no use for making lather, and the whole business was cold and wretched. My shoulder blades were covered with a sore rash, but I thought this was due not to lice but to the cutting of the straps.

Afterwards, Tich wanted us all to look smart for the funeral. Birch and I were the worst offenders – we had the least buttons on our coats and the most mud and tears on our trousers.

'You'll have to tidy up a bit,' said Tich. 'Joe's got the needle and cotton now, but you can have it when he's finished.'

At that moment I rather wished Tich wasn't an ex-quarter-master sergeant-major of the British Army but I changed my mind because he sewed on all my buttons and did the other repairs for me whenever I needed them. Much later, I discussed this with Babs, and said I thought the reason he had done this was partly good nature, and partly because it offended his mind to have anyone in our group looking untidy.

'No, it wasn't that,' said Babs. 'Tich liked you a lot. What he said was, he realized that what was a little thing to him, sewing on a few buttons, was more of a thing for you, and obviously a thoroughly disagreeable sort of job for you.'

We had a new lot of underwear, a shirt, sweaters, and a little bag with soap and shaving materials given out. Perhaps our old things were washed. I do not know, as we never saw them again. Whenever we came back for a rest from the front we were given a new set of clothing – we had everything new because our haversacks were continually being dumped in places and then lost. When I came back to England I reckoned that during the war I had left different lots of things first at Marseilles, then at Albacete, then Chinchon, then Fuencarral, then another lot at the Playa de Madrid, and another at Alfonso's palace, and another at Majadahonda, and another in a trench at Boadilla, and a full suitcase on my way back at Barcelona.

Louis Schuster – a famous German revolutionary, and our company's Political Commissar – was buried in the Moorish Mosque at Madrid. We were taken in by lorries and saw an air battle overhead on the way. Everyone came out of their houses to watch, and cheer the little red-winged Russian fighters against a squadron of heavy German bombers, escorted by fighting planes. The Germans were headed off; they circled round, dropped their bombs and returned; after that it was impossible to follow clearly, aircraft were flying regularly overhead for the next hour. We heard machine-gunning and saw one aeroplane crash. It was not terribly impressive, it was all over so quickly, a piece of flaming metal like a firework – we did not see it reach the ground. Later they told us two enemy planes were brought down. The best sight of all was the eighteen Russian fighters flying fast over-head in perfect formation, diving and zooming to salute the cheering population.

The funeral did not go off very efficiently. The firing of the final salvo was not unanimous, and a German song was interrupted by a gramophone record which played the Inter-nationale six times running. In spite of the inefficiency, perhaps even because of it, I shall always remember the scene – the vastness of the Mosque emphasized the littleness of the men standing, some rigidly at attention, others restlessly changing their position. From Max's speech I caught only a few phrases:

'Comrades – we have come here to Spain – Comrades to the last day, to the last man – we are fighting Hitler Germany. The real Germany of the German people will remember those who fought and died here. . . .' I thought of all these men, exiles. For them, indeed, there could be no surrender, no return; they were fighting for their cause and they were fighting as well for a home to live in. I remembered what I had heard from them of the exile's life, scraping an existence in Antwerp or Toulouse, pursued by immigration laws, pursued relentlessly – even in England – by the Nazi Secret Police. And they had staked everything on this war.

These men had been the front line troops of German socialism; some – veterans of the World War – had been through two revolutions in post-War Germany. They had known the horrors of Nazi concentration camps. With good reason, the Thaelmann Battalion had the reputation of being the finest fighting unit of the International Brigade. By the end of the year the battalion's strength had been filled up with French and Belgian companies, and today there can be only a few score of that trainload of cheering men that left Albacete in October. That afternoon at Schuster's funeral I could not bring myself to try to visualize and speculate on the future of these men, but I felt deeply for the first time a sense of the tragedy inherent in the very fact of these German volunteers – a tragedy almost as great as that of the Spanish war itself; a tragedy which beer fiestas and the coarse German character itself could never hide.

After the funeral, we had hoped to be allowed leave in Madrid. This became the main topic of conversation on the way back. That evening, we got our first lot of wages since Chinchon – a hundred pesetas each. We heard we were being paid at the regular 'active service' rate of the Spanish Army – ten pesetas a day.

'Shure, boy,' said Jerry, 'I saw something this afternoon I'd give the whole hundred for. Just wait till I get into that town, I shan't be back in a hurry.'

We got leave next day. Most of the battalion were taken in by lorry to go and have baths first in the town. Birch and I went in separately by tram. I had decided if we tried to find Sefton Delmer and Keith we should get a better bath that way and possibly a few free drinks and meals. The trams were very crowded, and we were encumbered by our rifles, which were constantly getting in people's way. Half-way we got out, and waved for a lift to a splendid Rolls-Royce flying an anarchist flag, which took us the rest of the way.

We found Delmer, several glasses of not very good brandy, and a gorgeous hot bath in the Gran Via Hotel. That bath was so excellent that I regarded it afterwards in the same light as a hot dish of eggs and bacon – as the highest of ideals to dream of when conditions were particularly bad. Birch said he did not want to meet Keith.

'Quite apart from what I think of him,' he said, while I was peeling off sweaters, waiting for him to finish washing, 'you seem to ignore the fact that he's working for a fascist paper.'

'But you don't really imagine the *Daily Express* is fascist?' I replied. 'I admit it's sensational, but it harms both sides; anyway, you've only got to compare it with the *Daily Mail* or *Morning Post*. . . .'

We carried this argument right on until I was in the bath at the ears and neck stage, and he was at the feet-drying stage. My main arguments were that there was a very capable Government censor; that the *Daily Express* was not banned, nor had its correspondents been expelled from Spain; that it had a reactionary, but at least democratic, policy. Birch said it was all the more venomous because it had not come out with an openly fascist policy; that it was absolutely typical of the English brand of hypocritical capitalism. We stopped before we started quarrelling.

Birch told me he was depressed by the English Group.

'They all want to go home, or most of them, as far as I can see,' he said.

I could see Birch was not only hypercritical and demanding an impossible standard in others (I had always thought he did this), but was genuinely miserable and disappointed. His single aim sincerity amazed me. I could see he would never begin to allow himself sympathy with those who couldn't keep his own high standard. Who else, I thought, was so unaffected? Keith

131

and Norman had found the first day too much; Bill had changed completely in the first three or four days of action – his face had got the bewildered expression of someone who is very cold and hopes to make himself warmer by drawing himself in. I had seen the same expression on Max's face when we left the White House. Max, whom we had all thought of as the very exemplification of Prussian militarism, had been quite broken now. Messer and I had agreed we didn't like war; even Ray had said we should have been relieved a day or two earlier; Babs and Tich and Jock and Joe all looked less tough now; Jeans was the only person I could place with Birch, and of the two he had less of the inhuman about him.

I was wrong in the way I figured everything out. Birch had showed he was more 'human' than anyone by the end. He was wrong, too, and misjudged a lot of the men just then. Because we grumbled and complained and cursed – and, indeed, seemed to occupy most of our time doing just these three things, it didn't mean we were demoralized. It only meant democracy in the Republican Army was something real.

✳

We had dinner in the Gran Via that evening. The food was a disappointment; we learned that the journalists regarded army rations as the height of luxury. We were introduced to the delegation of six M.P.s who were then on a visit to Madrid. Keith was there, too. As the brandy was consumed we heard any amount of war reminiscences; one Conservative member became very eloquent in expounding his ideas of how General Franco could have cut the Valencia road – or rather, how he could have done it himself, had he had a company of cavalry.

One gave me his address in London, and asked me to come and see him if I needed a job. Brandy made Birch talk communism steadily to a Labour member, whom he addressed as 'comrade'. Towards half-past ten we were the only people in the restaurant, and refugees were coming;

132

they spent the night rolled in blankets on the floor. I saw that it was too late for us to get back to our barracks that night, and also we had not got our rifles. We had left them in the journalists' living-room at the Telephone Building.

Birch was still arguing about politics when we got there. He shoved a cartridge into the breech, and swung the rifle round the room exclaiming, 'That's the only way – force – to deal with them.' We thought it would be fun to go along and try and sleep at the British Embassy, but then Birch pointed out that it would obscure the issues of the anti-fascist struggle, and he also mentioned that it would be a sectarian thing to do. So we went back to the hotel and the M.P. who had asked me to keep in touch with him offered to let us share his room. We went noisily upstairs, our host all the time exhorting us to keep quiet, as he particularly didn't want others to know we were sharing his room.*

In the morning, the M.P. insisted we should go down to breakfast five minutes ahead of him so that no one should think we had all spent the night in the same room. There was a cup of coffee and milk for each person and one roll, served by a gaunt, depressed-looking waiter. Another member of the delegation gave us three boxes of chocolates ('the last in Valencia') and whisky and Players cigarettes. They had a car, put at their disposal by the Ministry of War, which we commandeered to take us back to Fuencarral. Tich was the first person we saw. He looked disapproving, but became more friendly when I presented him with the spoils to divide up among everybody.

Jerry and Messer had come back ten minutes before. They

* This was the occasion referred to by Philip Toynbee in *Friends Apart*, pp. 95–6. The M.P. made a pass at Romilly and Birch. Romilly, profiting as usual from the unusual, extracted a promise from the M.P. that on his return to England he would publicly support the Republic, or else he would denounce him as a homosexual. The M.P. kept his part of the bargain, as did Romilly. The M.P. was killed in the War.

had spent the night at an anarchist cuartel; when Jerry saw the car we had come in he got the chauffeur to take him back into Madrid. He told us he was 'quitting'. I wasn't very surprised, and I hoped he would get out of the war, for which he was quite unsuited. 'You can't help liking the little blighter, you know,' said Babs.

Jerry was popular and could get away with a great deal. Birch and Jeans were the only ones who hadn't a good word for him. Jeans said to me: 'These people don't seem to realize the trouble and everything they cause ... Who's going to get them out of the country – how are they going to eat? I told Jerry last night the only way he could leave here was if he walked. There's a very serious petrol shortage; they don't seem to know what a war is ...'

Next day, Jeans asked me to have a word with him outside. 'I didn't want to say all I have to say now in front of every-one,' he said. 'Now I'm going to put a matter to you straight, though I was asked simply to make inquiries and find out, but I'd rather come to you direct. Are you Mr. Baldwin's nephew?'

He told me – after I had enlightened him about the relative of whom I seem to have become a kind of appendage – that there had been a lot of telegrams about me from my parents and others, and it had something to do with the War Office in Madrid. 'Anyway,' he added, 'the point is, if you want to go back to England you can do so now.'

Desperately glad though I had been to leave the Casa Velasquez, I hadn't the slightest wish to return to England then. That was all I heard about the matter.

There was less to buy in Fuencarral now – you could get black coffee at two places, but supplies ran out before eleven o'clock. There were no milk and no wine. Anis was about the only drink. There was wine to be bought in Madrid, but it was not a very exciting place to spend one's 'leave' in as it was quite dark after half-past five, no lights being shown for fear of air-raids. Birch and I were caught in a Metro station during one raid – we tried to get out on to the street, but a panic-stricken crowd made it impossible to move. The fear of suffocation was stronger than that of the bombs – women screamed and on the steps men were fighting to get inside the shelter.

As we heard the roar of the aero-engines overhead, I remembered the crowds gathered round the Metro station on our first day – bodies were still being excavated; two hundred people had been killed when an incendiary-bomb burst over a 'bomb-proof' shelter. Now there were twelve bursts – twelve explosions, each the signal for screaming hysteria – then silence. The suspense was no less terrifying, we could see nothing but a thick wall of panic-stricken men and women. Again the roar of engines, now closer, now we were ready for the next horrible crash. Now louder still, it must be the climax. The roar grew fainter; the raid was over.

I went with Aussie to an anarchist cuartel; they gave us ham and eggs and white wine and proper brandy. José showed me their manifesto – 'The Organization of Indiscipline', it seemed an admirable doctrine. We were soon very good friends and they promised to come and visit us at Fuencarral. I thought it would be amusing to let them have an argument with Birch. José and his friends made our leave in Madrid enjoyable – without them we should not have known what to do with ourselves – when you liked one of his cigarettes he gave you a dozen packets; if you were late going to barracks, he got hold of a Rolls-Royce to take you. Anarchists give the anti-fascist clenched fist salute with their left hand, and all of them wear conspicuous black and red caps or scarves. All the drivers of International Brigade lorries were anarchists.

At the barracks in Fuencarral, we had a lot to argue about; first of all, there was Oswald. Oswald had now been made Company Commander, and though everyone admired his courageous behaviour at the White House, his aggressive manner made him unpopular with the English. He was too inclined to imitate a Prussian sergeant-major, we thought. Babs proposed at a Group Meeting that we should recommend that an older and more experienced man should be appointed. 'I wouldn't take orders from a man like that,' he said. 'He can't control his temper. He seems to think this is a capitalist army, trying to make everyone jump up and salute or something silly.'

Eventually Walter became commander of our company, a man who everybody liked.

Another question was that of electing a 'political responsible'. At present we had difficulty in bringing up complaints because of our ignorance of German, and Jeans – being the zug leader – did not want to be always pestering the officers about Jock's pants or Sid's bad pesetas. These questions – trivial though they sound now – were all important to us.

A greater problem was that of our relations with the rest of the battalion. A lot of people felt there was not enough contact with the Germans. We now knew for certain that there was another group of about a dozen Englishmen who formed a machine-gun company in the Marseillaise French battalion, which had been stationed in the hospital building throughout the last action. Jeans inquired about the possibility of joining up with them, but for the moment it seemed impossible.

Jeans himself and Birch and people like Ray and Jock were completely happy staying as a small English Group with the Thaelmann Battalion. Joe and Aussie and Messer and I would have preferred to be in a Spanish regiment; Tich and Babs were with us to a certain extent in this, but they were chiefly concerned with joining the other English – as they could only speak one language. Very often when liaison was needed between the Thaelmann and French battalions, messages would be translated from German to English by Jeans and then from English to French by me.

We had told everyone of our extraordinary night with the M.P. Joe was delighted to hear there was an English delegation in Madrid and wanted to take us along to visit him the next time we were in Madrid.

'Well, I'm certainly not going about with that fat Joe,' Birch said to me. Joe spared no opportunity of turning his

136

flow of rhetoric to abuse of Birch, and there was a certain feud between the two. I had fortunately escaped Joe's attention for some time and got on quite well with him. Birch and Messer were my closest friends – though these two had not much to say to each other.

Joe and Tich and Jeans and Babs and Ray all had dinner with the M.P.s another night. Joe told us:

'When he asked, don't you know Wing-Commander James* (haw haw), what will you drink, I ordered a double brandy; does you good, boy, on a cold night like that. Afterwards when we were going out, I saw a car with a great Union Jack over it. F— me, I said, I'd like to know what that's doing here. So I shouted at the driver, halt there. A chap looks at me and says in a Park Lane voice, you know, top hat and all that: "What are you doing here, my man?" "Oh, I've been completing a few studies at the University, just up here for a vac." Then I asked him what he was doing and f— me if it wasn't the British ambassador or someone like that.'

Our relations with the English journalists in Madrid underwent a gradual change. At first they were delighted to see us; not only were English volunteers 'news', but we could give them a lot of information about the fighting in the University City. They were generous with drinks and cigarettes, but the limits of their generosity were severely tested, as we all lived off them. Jock was the worst offender, as he was always drunk after an hour in Madrid. Birch, too, took pleasure in getting drinks out of the journalists, whom he regarded as little better than fascists.

There was a fiesta which the Spanish communist party organized for the Thaelmann Battalion. We drank beer out of bottles steadily all through – and there were very good veal sandwiches. Afterwards Messer and I and Birch and Aussie thought we would go on for a little amusement somewhere else. We went to the Metro, but after a depressing wait, a

* Wing-Commander Sir Archibald James, Conservative M.P. for Wellingborough.

policeman came up and told us there was nothing much doing in the town after seven o'clock, so we went home.

I wrote a letter to my brother* at this time – I had wanted to write an article to send home, but I found it impossible to concentrate for long enough to put down more than a few words. It was easier to write a letter. I think I said something about the bad smell of dead Moors but this was the only discouraging note. My brother joined the British battalion which was formed at Albacete the following January. While I was ill with dysentery in Barcelona, he was travelling with other English recruits from Paris to Perpignan, and on through Barcelona to Valencia.

On the whole, Fuencarral was dull, but the nights were comfortable. We had no mattresses, but the school benches and blankets made good beds, and we never got up before nine in the morning.

On Sunday we had rifle practice. Max was in charge, as he had now been given a job as trainer and instructor, instead of leading the battalion in action. We were told that on the next day we would settle down to eight days' intensive training. It had always been intended by the Spanish Government to use the International Brigade as a mobile attacking force, to harass the enemy's flanks; so now we were going to be properly trained with 'manoeuvres'.

In the afternoon I walked over with Jeans to the armoury workshop, where we found Chris. He had turned out to be a first-class technician and spent his time repairing machine-guns. Now that he had recovered, he wanted to leave his job and join us as an ordinary militiaman, but the Germans would not hear of this. He was far too valuable. I showed him my rifle.

'Good heavens, man, the barrel's cracked,' he said. 'You'll blow yourself to bits if you fire that again.' He gave me a new one, which I marked with a knife on the wooden part

* This was Giles Romilly, who was then an undergraduate at Oxford.

of the barrel. I wrote: 'Romilly' and underneath, '3rd Zug, 1st Kompagnie Thaelmann.'

On the way back Jeans asked me if I'd like to go and have supper with a Spanish doctor and himself in Madrid that night. I looked forward to it. But an hour later an order came for us to get all our equipment ready. Jeans said he thought this meant for certain we were going somewhere else for our eight days' training. We grumbled at the lack of warning; everyone's kit was all over the place. Once more we went through the difficult manoeuvre of hoisting ourselves on to lorries, carrying rifles and blankets and haversacks and ammunition. The eight days' training was a pleasant myth. At dawn the next morning we were back in our old positions near the White House.

Chapter 11

There were picks and spades for everyone this time, and a German officer came to explain how to dig the trench to be safe from machine-gun strafing and shelling. I was working with Tich. 'Keep your head down,' he kept saying, 'you'll go having a nice good stretch and a bullet'll go clean through your head, and I shan't like that at all.'

It was a horrid morning. Either you shivered with the cold or sweated with the digging. We got to our positions an hour before dawn – and then for the first time we learned that the last battle had been in vain, that the White House was lost. We lay half an hour on the ridge behind the hospital building, with a thin spray of bullets passing overhead. Then, one by one, we crossed the road, passed the empty dug-outs which we had made two weeks before, went down into the valley and on to the ridge ahead. There were dug-outs here, shallow and sketchy things; we had to dig in properly. At twelve o'clock, when the day was at its hottest, Jeans said he would try to organize parties to rest in batches during the afternoon. But by the time we had finished the dug-outs and communication trenches, the officer arrived again and gave instructions for building a parapet with sand-bags. I went back and fetched a dozen bags – some were already filled, others we stuffed up with earth. The hardest job of all was to hoist the bags on to the parapet.

The company runner was an Austrian boy, who had been wounded in the arm during the very first action and had now come back from hospital. He was sent to take a message to the Clinic building. We saw him crouch by the road, then sprint across it. Ten yards beyond, he got to the cover of the rising ground and carried on slowly. We were all watching when he came back. His arms stretched forward, he sprawled over in the middle of the road, turned right over once, then lay there still.

A man dashed on to the road, got hold of his head and began to drag him into safety – then a bullet got him and they lay together a few yards from the side of the road. Jeans had been talking to Walter. He heard the wounded man shout, 'Sanitas, sanitas,' and picked up a stretcher. A lorry-driver got out of his car and came up the road to get hold of the other end. He was killed outright. Jeans got one of the men back, then half an hour later they brought up a tank to bring back the bodies of the driver and the Austrian boy.

There was no rest that night. They wanted us to dig a sap, stretching as far as fifty yards from the hen-house – that was where the fascist snipers were established. There was only room for one man to go in at a time and enlarge the sap, while another kept watch. When I began to dig I saw the mark from which the man before me had begun – I could never do all that amount – it was tempting to take three-minute rests, then five-minute rests, then rest the whole time. I worked with Jock. He was ideally suited to the job: 'Ay, ye have to have been a navvy, like me.' In half an hour he dug more than I could have done in two. He made the sap bend round. After an hour's spell there was another hour's ordinary guard duty to do. It was hard to keep awake, peering into the cold night, with a blanket wrapped up to one's chin. A flask of brandy made it easier. I only fired twice that night, though some men kept up a barrage the whole time. Dozing fitfully, we heard it, but though the enemy replied to the fire, no one stirred. At last the night was over, and the sap was finished.

When the sun came out at eight o'clock our spirits were better; we sat smoking and munching bully beef, and drinking coffee. There were twelve of us. Addley (Tich), Birch,

Cox, Gough, Jeans, Messer, Ovenden (Babs), Whateley and myself; Harry, the fat Swiss, had joined us as commander of the 2nd Group of Arnold's Zug; and there were two new recruits, a Londoner and an American, who joined us at Fuencarral just before the action. Dan, the first of these, was about twenty-three, and as cheerful and good-natured as Ray. But a week later, he went to hospital with appendicitis. The American was a much older, tough person, like an advertisement for an American insurance company. On this very morning, a piece of shrapnel from the fascist artillery got into his leg, and he went back to hospital.

As against these two, Jerry had gone. Keith and Norman and Donovan were long since forgotten. Chris was working in Fuencarral. Bill and Sid were ill somewhere in Madrid. So there were only twelve of us on the ridge with part of a Polish company on our right. The rest of the Thaelmann Battalion were spread out between the road and the Clinic Hospital, working hard at a long trench to join our whole line together.

That first day was warm and slack. Jeans asked for volunteers for an anti-tank squad again. There was little enthusiasm, but soon we all envied Babs and Ray and Harry, who got the job, as they were established in a natural cave made by the sloping ground at the corner of the road, and here they could smoke, keep warm, and even build a fire for heating coffee and food. That left nine of us to look after the ridge. Very often Jeans would be at a staff conference; three men would be fetching up rations; another might be obeying the calls of nature in the valley; another couple would most likely be paying a social call on the anti-tank squad; that left one man on guard, and another one sleeping in the sun to hold the ridge. Once there was no one there at all.

Jeans was away that afternoon on some mysterious mission. A night raid on the fort was expected. Birch was most affected by the news – he talked of nothing else, how he must manage to be included in it. He worried Jeans until the latter agreed to get a piece of paper and a pencil and write his name down. But he did not go. Twenty men under the command of Hans Beimler – political commandant of the Thaelmann Battalion – including Jeans himself and Jock, crept forward at eight o'clock. They had pistols and Mills bombs. Five minutes later half a dozen of the Balkan battalion on the right followed them. We were all ready and on the alert – waiting tensely, sometimes gazing over the parapets – but the sudden vicious clatter and flash of fire startled us. It was over in a few minutes, and Jock came panting back.

'Ay, lads, it was a raid; did ye no ken we were going on it? Ay, the—bastards, mucked it oop properly, they did. We got so close we could hear 'em talking, practically got right into their trenches there; ay, you know, right in front of the fort, they've been building them. Then those damned Polacks started chucking their stuff at us from behind.' The raid had failed. Hans Beimler was killed. His body has been buried in the Red Square of Moscow.

This raid was a turning-point for Birch. He brooded over the injustice of his exclusion; he became bitter and almost cynical.

I made friends with Joe; he was a useful person because he could always be relied upon to get extra supplies of food and coffee or extra blankets. We were both in charge of fetching food that week. Joe had lost his corduroy trousers somewhere in Madrid, and was now shivering in a pair of thin grey flannels. The morning after the raid, they brought up more equipment – steel helmets and gasmasks, and a pair of trousers for Joe. Joe got hold of a helmet with two heavy dents where bullets had grazed the metal. 'This'll do fine,' he said. 'You watch me march down the High Street of Luton with this.'

Over his specially appropriated supply of coffee and milk I asked him about his family in Luton. 'My brother, he's a bit slick,' he told me. 'You know, got a business of his own. I've never stuck to one thing, as you might say. You should have seen me at the Vauxhall works, though, they gave me the sack there, said it was for something or other; of course, really they found out I was in the Party. Then I went off to Germany – all round them blinkin' Youth Hostels and Hitler places – very decent they were, and I told them all I was a fascist. Oh yes, I give 'em the salute and all that, and all about Mosley; only one fellow says to me, "You know, you go on so how much you're for Hitler, I think perhaps you're not at all." He didn't mean it though, I don't think. . . . Here, catch hold of that coffee tin there, sounds like *"Fliege, Decke!"* '

'Fliege, Decke!' We heard this half a dozen times a day, always when we were resting or reading or chatting or digging – a tiresome interruption, while we watched the tiny specks in the sky. This time there was the same increasing drone that I remembered in the Metro station at Madrid – louder and louder. 'Eighteen of them, there's another three. . . .' They were passing right overhead. Like gigantic bats. 'Twenty-one, twenty-four, thirty, thirty-six. . . .'

We counted forty of them. It was the biggest air-raid yet – not on us, not on the artillery or fortifications behind, not on the transports and munitions and supplies, but on the thickly populated streets of Madrid. And I was glad at that moment – glad that they were attacking defenceless women and children, glad that those monsters had passed over us. Three hours later they came back again – killed twenty-five people in Fuencarral and hit the hospital six times. Now I understood why Spanish peasants had fled at the very sight of those monsters. That afternoon the sky was cloudless and we crouched in our dug-outs listening to the bombs and looking up to see the smoke belching into the sky in a score of different points behind us.

'There'll be no supper tonight,' said Jeans. 'The kitchen has been hit at Fuencarral, and it's very difficult on the road, as the bombs have made big holes. We must stay here tonight at all costs and tomorrow we may withdraw.'

That was a bad night, everyone jumpy, expecting attacks, talking of being cut off.

144

We knew Babs had got a whole pot of coffee in the anti-tank squad dug-out, so Joe and I went back to get some of this and see what else we could collect. By the time we reached the road, the first shots had been fired; in the darkness we could see the flash of rifle fire from our own trench, then the sharp whistle of bullets across the valley. We crouched down.'

'Vot zey do?' said Harry. 'Zey shoot at us. Zey are crazee.'

We waited ten minutes, while the firing got fiercer. I was worried. If there was an action, nothing was worse than being separated. I thought of that first grim night at Chinchon. The same thoughts occurred to all of us: there were only seven of them on that ridge, suppose it was the enemy who were there, who had killed them all, who were firing at us. The ridge bent round to the right so we could not see what was happening among the Poles. When the firing slackened, we crept back through the valley cautiously. They were all there. 'Just a strafing,' said Tich. 'Expect we'll have to get used to that sort of thing, about this time in the evening.'

We did; it was a regular occurrence every evening after this.

I said to Tich that night: 'I suppose this sort of trench warfare's something like the Great War, isn't it?'

He laughed. 'If you had the trenches dug properly, and if you had three miles of communication trenches, and a mass of saps running out, and firing steps, and pillar boxes, and barbed wire, it might be.'

'What was the longest you were at the front for?' we asked him.

'Of course, that depended on the type of place you were in. You might be in a salient where they couldn't bring up stuff and then you might be there up to thirty days; but then again, you had somewhere comfortable, and you knew just where you were. . . . Here!' (Tich suddenly noticed we had all gathered round to listen.) 'Whose turn is it, yours Cox, isn't it, to go on guard now? If you are all staying in the same spot here, you might get a bomb on the top of us all.'

But, he went on, 'You might be in a quiet spot three months and nothing happen. But if you popped your head over the top you'd likely as not get one. I know they made a lot of those attacks at the time, going over the top, but most times when you got there you'd find them all waiting with their hands up for you.'

Holding our blankets round to keep out the cold, talking in low whispers, sometimes peering over the parapet towards the outline of the White House, clear in the moonlight a hundred yards away, we asked Tich question after question about the Western Front of the Great War; what were the differences, which was worst, more dangerous, more exciting, more horrible? He said they had far more guns and planes and trench mortars and far more men and more trenches, but that this was equalized by the fact that they knew how to defend themselves better, how to be quite safe in deep dug-outs, that organization was better and hence there was far more feeling of security and safety, and that there was none of the frantic hand-grenade fighting from house to house and room to room – all that work of penetration was done by the heavy guns behind. Another important factor was the fact that you could be taken prisoner – there was none of the bitter, relentless 'No quarter' attitude which characterized this war.

'As far as I'm concerned,' said Tich, 'this is a war we know all about, we all know what we're fighting for and why we're fighting.' We lacked the organizational ability, the perfectness of the British Army, but we lacked also its repressive discipline. 'I remember one chap we had in our company in 1915,' said Tich. 'He was a prisoner, though we never knew what he'd done. I expect really what it was, he was serving a sentence and they let him out. He was free in the trenches, we only knew how it was about him when we went back for a rest, for as soon as we'd got out of the reserve lines they put him in handcuffs. Then when we had time to spare after stand-to in the morning, he'd have to work. I could see he was getting desperate all right, going on like this, month after month; and one morning when we were up the front, and the sergeant's back was turned, he got over the parapet and ran as fast as he could. I think he wanted to finish himself off, though he may have thought he'd get to the German lines and surrender. When he got over the other side, a dozen Germans were sitting waiting and stuck their hands up to him. So he got a decoration and his sentence remitted, of course, and everything. . . .'

The night passed, and next morning there was complete calm again – the White House seemed to be deserted. Jeans told us, 'We have to be very quiet today, and observe the enemy. No careless shooting.' We pressed him to say what all this meant till he got irritated. 'All I can do is translate this order; go and ask the general.'

Messer was hit by a stray bullet that day – it shaved the skin off his balls. 'It's all right, chaps,' he shouted as he went back to the Red Cross Station, 'you can envy my luck.' After that we were more careful about walking behind the trench – for a few hours, until we got tired of bending double. Messer's absence was very noticeable because he was one of the hardest workers.

Jerry turned up an hour later. 'This is some sort of a bum racket, ain't it,' he asked. 'I figured on how you chaps'd be warming up the kippers in that White House – what did they do, chuck you out o' there?'

We asked him what had happened to him in Madrid, why he had decided to come back, or who made him come back.

'No, I sure came back here of my own free will,' he said. 'Them guys up there, they got me guessing, they don't give a man a fair chance, they wanted to know what I was doing and why and all that, they got me all twisted. They had me guarding trucks a day or so – I reckoned as how I was better off back here than all tied up with that bunch guarding trucks, so here I am.'

I told him about Messer. 'Shure, that's reg'lar bad, that's a reg'lar good fellow,' he said – Messer was Jerry's best friend. He shared Aussie's dug-out that night.

When Jerry's second turn on guard came along, he refused to get up. Half asleep, I listened to the argument. Aussie was speaking: 'A man's got to stick to the rules the same as anyone else. I'll go on now, but the man's no good at all.' Then Tich, quieter, 'Well, we'll have to make everyone have an extra spell, that's all, you carry on for a quarter of an hour, Aussie, and I'll wake Romilly up to relieve you. We'll see about it tomorrow, you can be sure.'

Next morning, we saw about it. Tich explained what had happened, and it was unanimously agreed to ask Jeans to have Jerry sent back to Madrid once more.

Jerry told us he had been ill during the night – he had toothache, he could not get up, he had a headache, he promised such a thing would never occur again. Then Jeans came along and said, 'Come on, Jerry, you can go back on the food lorry.'

'You guys have got me wrong,' he said. 'That's a thing might happen to anyone. You've got me wrong.' So Jerry stayed.

There were no more night raids that week and we settled down to the routine of eating, sleeping, improving the dug-outs and communication trenches and the sap, watching the air-aids and listening to the heavy pounding of the big guns behind and in front. The only diversion was an experiment with a new kind of trench mortar they brought up. Jeans and Jock were the only ones who knew how to make it work; when they pulled the wire, we leaned over the parapets to watch where the bomb landed, and shot at anyone we saw after the burst.

'That's asking for trouble, I call it,' said Joe. 'You start playing about with that kind of thing and they'll give you the same medicine; can't say we wouldn't deserve it, either, starting up that infernal thing when we're all nice and quiet here.' I quite agreed with him.

We tried to stop Jock dragging the machine out every time

we were trying to sleep in the sun. An enemy plane circled menacingly overhead.

'There you are,' said Joe. 'That's your fault, Jock, go on now, stand up and own up you did it now, or he'll punish the whole class.' But the nearest the bomb ever got was into the valley behind us.

The weather grew colder and we had a rainstorm which was worse than an artillery bombardment. After that we never recovered our good spirits, and began to talk of being relieved. Harry looked most miserable in the cold wet weather. I asked him if it wasn't as cold as that in Switzerland. 'Yez, but zere is not zees awful damp,' he answered. 'Now I have zee cramp in my stomach.'

Next morning Harry's fat kind face was wrinkled with pain, and he went back to hospital. We all wanted to take his place in the anti-tank squad, though Babs said, 'Yes, you weren't so keen when you thought there was any chance of seeing a tank, were you? Christ knows what we'd do if we did see one. . . . You wait till you've sat there quaking in your shoes while they're dropping bombs – that whole place might fall in on you. Another thing; we've got longer guard spells: hour and a half on and three hours off at night. Then there's all the day to be done as well, I mean, you don't exactly need a regular guard the whole time, but someone's got to be there, on the alert, you can see that. And then old Harry, he's all right I know, but if he gets a bit of sun he'll go to sleep in it. That means at about four or five o'clock in the afternoon, I might be out here, and Ray might want to have a sleep or something and he can't, same way if he's on some job and I'm there, I've got to keep awake the whole time.'

Birch took Harry's place. That same day Jeans told us we would be relieved at seven o'clock in the evening. Seven o'clock came and eight o'clock and nine o'clock. Birch and Babs and Ray came back from their dug-out, we heard the Poles moving off and the rest of the Thaelmann Battalion, and still no order came for us to move. We had our packs and blankets done up and stood about waiting. A few bullets from the White House made Jeans exclaim, 'Good heavens, isn't anyone watching?'

'It's your turn, Birch,' said somebody.

'No, it's not,' he answered. 'I'm always volunteering for things and I'm just about sick of it; anyway, I'm in the anti-tank corps, so someone else can do it.'

Chapter 12

The Playa de Madrid, where we went for a few days' rest, was once the smartest road-house and night-club for wealthy Madrid week-enders. It had four bars, a restaurant, a park drive, a tennis court, a miniature golf links, a river with canoes and paddle-steamers.... When we got there it was just as the owners had left in October when they joined the everlasting trek back to the capital. Dirty teacups and plates and knives, with little square tables and chairs standing out in the sun, half-empty bottles of gin and anis. For our quarters we had what was once a room for light refreshments. I shared a bed, made up out of two planks from a canoe, behind the bar, with Joe. Next day, they brought mattresses.

We ate our breakfast at tables with tablecloths with neat little places and paper napkins and plates and cups. Tich organized everything. After six hours' hard sweeping and cleaning, we had a comfortable living-room and dining-room. Perhaps, before the war, tired business men brought their girl friends to the Playa de Madrid to forget their cares in luxury and rest. Though there were no girl friends and little luxury, the Playa was a haven for us, too. We could sit on a sun roof smoking cigars, or take out a boat on to the river, or gather round the table to play poker, with cups of steaming hot coffee at our side – it was the nearest we had got to comfort and civilization.

'You coming along for a little, ah, boating?' asked Joe. We dragged an old tub from the bank and started punting up the river. The water was ice-cold.

Jerry was in a little paddle-steamer by himself. 'You guys

seen Jock?' he shouted, 'that fellow's sure soused!' We looked round, and saw Jock panting along the bank, like a dishevelled spaniel. 'Coom on Jerry,' he was calling. 'Be a sport, I'll show you how to row a boat.'

Jerry steered dexterously away – our punt was drifting in a current towards the bank, and I was afraid Jock would see us in a minute. He did.

'Ay, there, it's you, Romilly,' he floundered into the water towards us. 'Ay, d'ye see how I'm the champion paddler. . . .'

He pulled up his trousers and waded in further, clutching in the air towards us. His face lit up when he saw Joe behind me. 'Ay, ye can't steer it, let Jock coom in the boat and show you.'

I expected a keenly disputed match of repartee. But Joe brought the barge pole firmly into the mud, splashing Jock, and sending us out into mid-stream again. 'I can't swim,' he told me. 'I think we'll leave Jock to someone else.'

Jock was standing puzzled, with the water up to his knees – then he stumbled back and ran along the bank to find Jerry again.

When we came back, an hour later, Jock and Jerry were both huddled up in blankets with their clothes drying in the sun. Jock was snoring heavily in a corner of the room. Whenever he rolled over and began talking, he was the centre of sarcastic inquiries about his health.

'Sure, I pushed that guy in,' said Jerry sadly. 'Only he got hold of me and I went in, too.'

Birch pushed his way to Jock, carrying a cup of coffee.

'Walter's told me to take charge of Jock,' he said. 'So no one's to talk to him now or gather round him.'

'You—,' from Joe.

'That guy's off his crackers,' from Jerry.

Next meal, Birch wanted us all to bet him he could not take ten glasses of wine without getting drunk. I bet him five pesetas. At the end he explained to us the theory of relativity – and also the connection between Marxism and the splitting of the atom; as he was a scientist, the jury hesitated to say whether he was drunk. Eventually they decided he had lost – but he did not agree. The last thing he said that night was that he hated humorous, cynical people. After that, things got worse. We had an argument about the rival merits of Englishmen and Scotchmen – Jock talking the most; Birch said he was related to the Campbells, so Jock told him these were the 'stinking billies' of Scotland. Remembering I had been a Jacobite four years before I joined in with him. Jock was launched into a real slanging match. Birch chose his words carefully; he was very annoyed, going from the general to the particular.

Strolling in the garden afterwards, I said to Birch, 'You know, I hope you won't mind my saying, but you oughtn't to take all that rot of Jock's (and mine for that matter) seriously; you seem to think everyone's against you.'

'Go to hell and leave me alone,' was his answer.

We played poker, and Jerry and I each won 150 pesetas. Birch lost all his money, and I lent him forty to go on playing with. During the game, we all got paid 200 pesetas as wages and they took a collection for the Red Cross. Most of us gave fifty or seventy-five. Birch gave the whole 200.

I took a fifty-peseta note from my winnings on the table and said to him: 'Take this from me in your contribution, and keep fifty.'

'You can give that if you like, extra,' he said. 'I don't want it.'

Each zug took it in turn to do twenty-four-hour guard duty – that meant two men patrolling the grounds of the Playa at night and one during the day. Joe and I did our spell together – we had three lots of an hour and a half that night – it meant we didn't wake each other up. Jeans joined us on the first spell. It was a bitter cold night; I asked him to get me a pair of fur gloves if he went to Madrid – the ones they gave us were too tight and thin to give any warmth.

'We'll get leave, won't we?' asked Joe. 'We ought to anyway. What's the good of this dough, if we don't, silly sort of idea to give it to us now.'

153

Jeans told us the military situation was very serious; the air-raids were getting worse. 'I've just been talking to an officer in a very high position,' he said. 'There's a chance the fascists may get into Madrid at any moment. Franco may sacrifice Burgos to get Madrid. So, you see, what with that and the air-raids, they want as few soldiers on leave in Madrid as possible now. You know, Joe, we're not supposed to be resting here. . . .'

'Well, we've been doing it for a couple of days,' I interrupted.

'Yes, you see,' he told us, 'that is somebody's fault for saying it wrong. We are here for three days in reserve. Any moment we may be called up to the front. Our flyers have seen great signs the fascists are moving up all their troops and lorries for another attack. You know it is supposed we should all be ready in ten minutes. Walter asked me this afternoon where we all were, some were on the river, and Harry was asleep on the bank the other side when he was supposed to be on guard. . . . I think it's likely we might be called up to the front tonight.'

We reached the maingate and tramped on to the road. We stood still and listened. Away in the night came the sound of battle – the steady clatter of machine-guns in the distance. It made the war a reality as much as fighting. There was something sinister in that sound. One wanted to creep indoors to the warmth and snuggle up and shut the door on it. An ambulance car flashed past us without lights.

We left the Playa that night, and spent another four days at the same front. The place was filthy by now – full of old tins and refuse and paper – the valley between the road and the front line positions was a bin for everything and a lavatory for the troops. There was no attack – and very little sun those four days. We returned to the Playa.

'Let's have a game of tennis,' said Jeans. 'I expect there's an old racket or two somewhere. I've found a ball.' We were standing at the main gate, waiting for the food lorries at seven o'clock in the morning. Jeans had told me I'd been

154

appointed food commissar, as I knew a little German. It entailed getting up at seven to collect the rations for our zug.

'I hope it'll be better now,' he said. 'There's been too much misunderstanding about this question. But now we have this new man it will be better. Only, you know, we mustn't all snatch or "organize" stuff; you can't do anything that way.'

We carried the coffee pot between us, then I went back to fetch the bread and butter and marmalade.

'That's good stuff, that,' said Joe. 'Here, boy, cut a slice off, we'll put it in our private larder behind the bar.'

After lunch Joe and I set out to find some eggs and milk. We crossed a bridge, climbed over a barbed-wire fence, and made for a farm half a mile away.

'Hoy, there,' Joe shouted to an old woman pottering about with a bucket of chicken food in her hand. 'You got milk, you know, Leche, Leche, and any *hweevos*.'

She poured out a jug of cold milk, and took us to the parlour, where we introduced ourselves to the family – half a dozen old aunts and uncles. She put the jug down on the table and stood still for a second. Fear was in her eyes. 'Aeroplanes,' she whispered. 'Listen! Trimotors! Germans!'

Then we heard the drone in the distance, and went out to gaze up into the sky; they did not go over the farm, it was only another raid on Madrid. We returned to the Playa.

'That woman must have had some time here,' said Joe. 'Why, she knew those were Junkers before I even heard 'em.'

A group of anarchists had come to visit us. We argued about the war, Russia, and politics and philosophy. They told us their leaders had joined the Government (of which they disapproved) only till the end of the war, to help to win, and because it was the only way their soldiers could get food and equipment. In spite of this we envied their present equipment. They were as 'light' as we were 'heavy'.

Aussie said to me when they had gone: 'Those fellows took to Joe, you know. They all liked him. I reckon all these

155

Spaniards do,' he chuckled. 'You find the same if you get among the Mexicans; the one crime among those fellows is to tell a man to shut his mouth. They can't have too much talk. Joe's lost among English and German people. You see him in Madrid; he can shout all the nonsense he wants; they like it.'

Next day Joe and Aussie and Jerry and I decided to have a day in Madrid. Jeans had said: 'Don't go and do anything silly and we'll arrange something all right in a day or two.' But we were impatient, so we did something silly.

They took us in lorries to Madrid for baths in the morning, and we made our escape when they halted for a procession. We asked the way to the Gran Via, and a beautiful young blonde accompanied us. It came as a shock when we found she had left us.

'That's your fault, Joe,' said Jerry. 'Too much arm work, moving your hands up and down all the time you speak; she gets kinda scared. Whoeu, that was some kid, I'd sure give a whole 500 for her.'

'How much money have you got, Jerry?' I asked.

'I got enough to get along with. You're a sap handing out all your poker winnings; you oughter stick to that dough; it'll come in handy all right. Don't you believe that talk about the stuff being no good. I'll take any you don't want!'

We met Messer in a café. He gave us his news.

'I had a grand time all right for a week in hospital,' he said. 'Coffee with milk every morning, and wine, and better grub than that tinned stuff. The Spaniards run it, and they know more about cooking than these Germans. Now I've got to come in here every day for treatment. I'm getting sick of it; in fact, I shouldn't have come in at all only I thought I'd find out where you chaps were, and come back and join you.'

Then I saw a figure winding its way through the tables towards us. It was Keith. He looked a bit glum when he saw how many of us there were. 'I was going to say you could have lunch here,' he said. 'You know they've got a

156

new rule about this place only being for the Press – special order from the War Ministry. They're feeding up the Press boys properly now; they've just turned out a couple of fellows in militia uniform.'

After a lot of arguing with the gaunt old waiter, in which there was much reference to the 'comrade who had been wounded', we got some lunch. It was not so good as our rations. Sitting at another table with a group of English journalists was David Mackenzie; he was a member of the British machine-gun group attached to the Marseillaise Battalion. 'I've come here to deny the report that I've been killed,' I heard him saying.

We compared a few experiences together. They had been in the Clinic building while we were attacking the White House. . . . 'I know all about you,' he told me, 'from one of our chaps who knows you.'

'Who's that?'

'John Cornford.'*

I had met John Cornford when I was fifteen and trying to start a public schoolboys' anti-war paper at Wellington College. Mackenzie told us all their group had asked for a transfer from their battalion to join us. They thought the Germans were easier to get on with than the French. I thought the reverse, but I didn't say so.

After lunch Keith asked me to go along with him to the Model Prison. 'There's a block of disused flats there where you can see the Clinic and all the other buildings. I've always wanted to go there. We can probably pick something up. I got a radio the other day like that.'

Keith showed me his passes from the War Ministry.

'Didn't you have any difficulty in getting them?' I asked.

'No, well, of course I told you I'd had a talk with Van Renn and he was very decent and gave me a letter, and then

* John Cornford, a communist and very promising poet, was the son of the classics don F. M. Cornford and the poet Frances Cornford. See, for him, *Journey to the Frontier,* a memoir by Peter Stansky and W. Abrahams (London, 1966).

it was easy. Delmer's in England now, so I've got a good deal of work.'

We passed the prison, went down barricaded streets, and sprinted across a square ('They've got a machine-gun there'), and climbed four flights of a block of flats where the walls were plastered with shell-holes. I picked up a kettle, several packets of peppermint tea, a grey woollen sweater (which I wear today) and a silk cushion. Incidentally this is the only case of looting I ever saw in the war – and these flats were two hundred yards from the battle front.

By the evening we were all depressed. 'Just tell 'em the truth, that's all there is to it, boy,' said Joe. 'Just say we didn't get leave so we took it,' but his words didn't comfort me much.

Messer came with us. It was ten o'clock and we were quite exhausted by the time we got back to the Playa. A guard challenged us. He was a Spaniard. That was our first inclination that something was wrong. We ran from the gate to the café and tiptoed in so as to wake no one up. The place was empty and our packs, helmets and gasmasks and rifles were gone.

Joe and Jerry and Messer were all arguing loudly. Aussie broke in: 'What's the use of going on like that? We'll be all right here for the night. These chaps are anarchists. They've got a different point of view on this discipline question.'

He was right. Aussie explained to the commandant what had happened, and they gave us a hot meal, and blankets to sleep under. Next morning, they told us to go in one of their lorries and try to find our battalion. The people at the kitchen depot in Fuencarral would know. Perhaps they had gone up to the front. . . . The Spaniards laughed at our unfortunate situation and did their best to cheer us up.

We got to our new headquarters – a lovely old castle, once used by Alfonso's son – the other side of Fuencarral near Las Rosas, at eight o'clock. We brought up the morning rations and tried to pass the matter off as lightly as possible.

'Hullo, Tich,' I said. 'Look here, I've brought some packets of peppermint tea, and Joe bought some sausages we can cook.'

But Jeans said, 'This is very silly, you know. I'll tell you, there were two chaps came back last night, and they spent the night in the lock-up here.'

I was relieved to find my rifle and pack stacked up against the wall. (We were occupying what were once no doubt servants' bedrooms – there were two adjoining rooms, each with two beds and chandeliers hanging from the ceiling; it was very grand.)

I could see we were all set now for a really big row – but it was bigger than I expected. It started in the 'cell' (a disused cloak-room) where we were all four 'detained' together with three or four Germans who had also taken leave in Madrid. Two Germans were set to guard us, but all was quite friendly and we smoked and read newspapers.

'Well, boy,' said Joe, 'we can't complain about this, you know; it's what we expected. But I'm not going to do any work.'

'You don't want to talk so big,' said Jerry. 'I guess them guys'll have you up before a court martial; you don't know where you are with this bunch of Square Heads.'

One of the guards, a stocky Prussian with whom there had always been a certain mutual dislike, overheard this remark.

Jock and Babs and Messer came into see us and brought us a tin of peaches.

'You chaps all right?' said Messer. 'We've just had a grand chin-chin about it with old Richard (the new commandant of the Thaelmann Battalion).* You know, spirit of voluntary discipline and all that, and then he said he wanted to let the culprits off; but it turns out that these three other chaps, the Germans, have been in trouble of some sort before, always wanting to get away from the front and all that, and it was their own bloody lot that said they ought to be

* A German communist whose real name was Staimer.

159

punished. Then Richard said he couldn't punish them without punishing the whole lot, so that's that.'

'You won't get much,' said Babs. 'Extra guard duty, I expect, anyway, you've missed one parade.'

At this point the guard came up and said the prisoners weren't allowed visitors.

'See you later,' said Jock.

Joe's face flushed. 'The f— b—s,' he muttered. 'Ask him who he's getting his orders from, and who told him to say that.'

The trouble had started. I had a long argument with the guards in French – it made relations worse. A Spanish lorry-driver came into the room, looking for a macintosh coat. We had spent some time with him in Madrid. He gave us each a packet of cigarettes, and Aussie showed him the newspaper. That was the signal for the explosion. The guards told him to move off. Joe gave the Spaniard a rapid insight into his views of the German nation in general. I interpreted a good deal, and added a good deal more of my own. One of the guards went to fetch Oswald. Then they tried to get Joe locked up in a cubicle, the size of a cupboard off the cloak-room. Some more Germans arrived, and one of them produced a pistol.

The whole thing lasted perhaps two minutes from the time the Spaniard had given us the cigarettes. At the end of it we were under double guard, the guards had all loaded their rifles, and Joe's lip was bleeding profusely where someone had struck him with the butt of a rifle.

There was an inquiry that evening. Joe was bandaged and furious – so were we all. The inquiry smoothed matters over a little. I interpreted for the others. The commandant asked if we admitted the gravity of our offence in going to Madrid without leave. I said yes. He said, good, we had been punished for that, and it was settled. He then said he would inquire as to whose fault the incident in the cloak-room had been and that anyone who was found guilty of unprovoked assault would be punished. We admitted one of us might have remarked, as was alleged, that 'the Germans were nothing better than fascists.'

'Certainly,' shouted Joe. 'Certainly that's what I mean too.' And then, in a lower tone, 'These muckin' Fritzies they go on about how marvellous they are, and their *genossen* this and *genossen* that, and what a lot they know about fighting. Anyone'd think, to hear 'em talk, they'd won the muckin' War, only it was the muckin' English that happen to have muckin' well beat them.' Fortunately no one heard or understood much of this.

At the end Richard said that we three – Joe, Aussie and myself, who were 'good comrades' – could return to our group, but Jerry was to be kept under guard for the present. He referred to Jerry as 'the Italian comrade, against whom we have heard other complaints'. This made a new diversion. I translated what he had said, and then announced that we wanted to know why there was discrimination against Jerry. Richard said that the English group had said they did not want him. Finally, he let him go too.

We talked late that night. Irritation and bad feeling had practically reached its peak. There were two major rows. Joe's lip and Jerry.

They held the inquiry, and afterwards we had a Group Meeting at which Walter (the Commander of the 1st Company) and Herbert (the new Political Commissar for the company) attended. Both were popular. Walter was a tiny little man with a roguish smile and a lisp in his speech. We had got to know and like him during our two quiet spells opposite the White House.* Herbert was the same age – no more than thirty – dark, shaggy, and Jewish. He had been appointed at the Playa, but it was his dealing with this 'incident' which made him really liked. He asked us if we wanted to have the news read first or whether we should discuss personal questions; we decided on the news. It was

* Not to be confused with 'General' Walter, the *nom de guerre* of the Polish communist Swierczewski who shortly became commander of the XIVth International Brigade.

all about the arrival of 25,000 German troops in Rebel Spain; the last item said reliable reports stated a large batch of these had been sent up to the Madrid front. Then Herbert said he would ask all of us to tell him our versions of the incident when Joe had been hit. 'Could you point out the people in an identification parade?' he asked.

The discussion went on three hours. Everyone took a hand. Tich said that at all costs they must avoid a division of feeling as between English and Germans, but that as a group they felt Joe had been badly treated and that therefore they had supported the investigation. Birch said he was disgusted by the attitude of some of the English comrades, that he had only the sincerest feelings of admiration for every one of the Germans, and that, in the event of any sort of split, he would like to fight as an individual German in the Thaelmann Battalion. But Herbert and Raymond Cox solved the difficulty. Ray jumped up after Jerry had been speaking. 'Wait a minute, Jerry,' he said. 'The important thing is Joe said a few minutes ago he was prepared to shake hands and make the whole thing up. Romilly and Aussie said so before. Isn't that so, Joe? Comrades, we must stop this quarrel.'

The peak had been reached, and that was the end of the row. I have described everything about it because it was important to us at the time – as important as any fighting – and because it is obvious there will be rows – rows between individuals and rows between groups and rows between nationalities – in such a diverse collection of men as the members of the First International Brigade. It was the only serious 'incident' that I ever saw. And after that quarrel was settled, relations grew steadily better all round, and by the time we left for the front again, no one was outside the general feeling of goodwill. The irritation had worked up to its peak, there had been an explosion, and we all felt better for it afterwards.

The agreeable comfort of the mattresses and blankets and warm rooms of the castle was conducive to good feeling. In the hall outside was a big wooden fireplace, and here we sat in the evenings, talking, smoking and roasting chestnuts. We had a ration of raw eggs and Tich fried them for us on the open fire.

'Well, we knew what we were in for here,' he said; 'but I know I'll be glad when this thing's over.'

'Christmas soon, boy,' said Joe. 'I wouldn't mind just sitting down to a nice bit of Christmas pudding with my old woman, she knows how to make it all right.'

'D'you wish you were back, Joe?' I asked.

'Wish I was, that I do. Mustn't though, not till we've finished this job. Wouldn't mind just popping back for a week at Christmas, though.'

The kettle of water was boiling, and we drank cups of the peppermint tea. It wasn't very nice.

'Wonder how long this business is going to last.'

'Of course we're in a different position from these Germans here – they've got no homes to go back to at the finish.What's going to happen to them poor devils.'

'I can't see it, honestly I can't, how this is going to finish. Look at all the stuff the fascists have got, all them German aeroplanes and tanks and guns. It's a blooming stalemate, that's all it is.'

'Poor old Harry, he's feelin' the cold all right. He was sayin' to me about all these new Hitler troops coming in – '

'Nah, you can't believe all that stuff they say, that's just propaganda.'

'You should hear the way the Fritzies were carrying on, you know, *genossen* and all that, and how they're all pleased and proud to meet the Hitler troops and have a good stab at them. More than I am. These Moors are bad enough, but you get properly trained German troops and you're really up against something. We knew that in the War, didn't we, Tich?'

'Damn fine fellows those Germans here are; give Hitler's boys a hiding all right.'

'I'll say they are. . . .'

'Any tea left for me?' Jeans pushed his way through the

circle and rubbed his hands in front of the fire.

'Well, Tich,' he said, 'I congratulate you, you're a sergeant now, so they'll all salute you on parade.'

He explained there was a new order by which the militia and the International Brigade were washed out, and we were all incorporated in the regular Spanish army. 'That means,' he went on, 'we have to get up quicker in the morning now; in the Spanish army a man has four minutes to get up and get washed.'

This change was the signal for yet more announcements about intensified militarization, better discipline and efficiency, training and manoeuvres. We were a little sceptical. We had heard all this before some time. Babs was muttering: 'It's all right for you young chaps, all these physical jerks in the morning. I'm too old to start that sort of thing at my time of life. I came out here to fight bleedin' fascism. I didn't come to have a soldier made of me. What do you think, Tich?'

But this time a few things did happen. First we had gas-mask instruction. I could not understand much of it, and I never managed to get my mask fitted on properly without someone to help me. Jeans told us that there were apparently four kinds of gases. I think he said one was mustard gas, which wasn't very serious, but the other three were all fairly bad. Then there was liquid gas. 'If you get any of this on your hands or anywhere, you must go back at once to find the *sanitas* people and they will put a special preparation on.' (We laughed. Joe said: 'I suppose if you want those *sanitas* people you ask a policeman where they are.')

The rest of the time was spent in an argument between Jeans and Birch, who insisted that no provision had been made for a fifth kind of gas, more deadly than the others.

'No, but seriously,' Jeans said at the end of the demonstration, 'there are four men in hospital in Madrid, and this doctor here – I saw him just now – says they are suffering from fumes from gas shells.'

We had three days of manoeuvres. It was beautiful country,

164

and the weather was always sunny but not too hot. Those three days were the most enjoyable of any we had in Spain. The first day Jeans said to me: 'Romilly, you can be the zug runner if you like, as you know French and German.'

'That'll suit me fine,' I answered. 'That means no digging, I hope.'

We staged an elaborate attack on a red brick house on the horizon. In my first attempt at keeping liaison I got lost and turned up at the wrong house. A family was having lunch. They gave me a glass of wine and I stayed and chatted.

Then I found Walter and took a message from him to Rickard. It said: 'We have obtained all the positions mentioned. The enemy left twelve dead on the field, and a great quantity of machine-guns, rifles, ammunition, etc.; we took three prisoners, who gave details of the demoralized state of the enemy' – this was all great fun.

After lunch we had target practice – Harry and Tich were the best of our group. 'Not bad, our score,' said Joe. 'Not bad for a young group like this.'

We had one more day's leave in Madrid, when I discovered a large library of English and American books. Madrid was gloomy and I saw a man's head almost blown off by a shrapnel shell. It was nice to get back to the castle.

Joe and I got permission to go for a long walk in the country. We took wine and rolls of bread with us, and were given fried eggs at a little farm. Sometimes there were aeroplanes in the sky, but they did not disturb the serenity of the day. We walked through the woods of El Prado, skirted Fuencarral, and got briskly down country lanes to the peaceful little town of Aravaca. On one side the country rolled on flatly past the green-brown plain of Madrid – it was small beside the towering snow-capped peaks of the Guadarrama mountains behind us. We forgot the war. It was cold and dark when we trudged up the last half-mile from El Prado to the gravel drive of the castle.

✳

When we got back Jerry was there to meet us.

'I guess I nearly missed you guys – that would have shure been awful as I guess you two and old Aussie and Messer have just about been my best pals here. . . .'

Jerry was leaving by lorry early next morning – he was being transferred to work in a munitions factory at Barcelona.

Jeans told us: 'I didn't know Jerry hasn't been well, and his accident' (Jeans was referring to Jerry's two missing fingers) 'makes it more difficult, now they've fixed up this job for him it'll be better altogether.'

I was sorry to say good-bye to Jerry – his wise-crackings, tolerant individualism was a relief from the eternal grimness of the war. And Jerry had no politics; that was an important thing.

The training went on – we were told about rocket signals that meant gas attacks, and other signals for advancing and signals for retreating. There was a rumour we would be going to Toledo to attack the rebels in the rear as a mobile column. Birch was very pleased. 'At last, we'll have something to show for ourselves,' he said. 'We haven't done anything yet worth speaking of. We'll be able to prove what we're worth at last.'

During these days I realized that for all his faults (faults of growing intolerance, of frigid remoteness from his companions), Lorrimer Birch possessed all the qualities of a revolutionary. He had that cold intellectual force which enabled him never to swerve from one straight path; he had the qualifications of a communist martyr.

Chapter 13

We never went to Toledo. A fortnight before Christmas we left the castle one afternoon and spent the night at the village of Majadahonda. Ours was its first military occupation, so I suppose this was the first genuine, muddy, Spanish village I had seen. A little boy told me excitedly about all the tanks and armoured cars they had seen going through to the front. We had to wait a long time for accommodation. While we were waiting, I talked to Tich and Babs, and again I wished Tich was in charge of organizing everything. Then Jeans told us we were going to sleep in a comfortable hotel. Walter had found the old woman who owned it. She said her husband was away, and she didn't know where the key was.

Walter tried to persuade her to recall its whereabouts for half an hour or so. Then he gave orders for the door to be smashed in. Then she found the key. But in the end the hotel and all its beds were reserved for the staff and medical people, and we had one room in a little house. Joe went down to see what he could organize in the kitchen, and I spread out our blankets in a corner. There wasn't much room, and it was a good time before everyone was settled. When Joe returned, he brought a thermos, a coffee heater and a frying-pan with him. We talked late that night.

Jeans brought a map, and drew in the positions of the Government lines to the west and north-west of Madrid. We were depressed at seeing it – the rebels had a much wider salient than we had managed. Our vital point was the Escorial road. But then the whole war has been full of vital points –

points 'commanding towns', or 'dominating roads', or 'surrounding enemies' flanks', or 'menacing communications', which have turned out in the end not to be vital at all. The mistake has been made by 'military experts' who, writing in the papers, have seen the whole thing in the same light as the Great War. But the important difference is that in the Great War there were strongly organized 'lines', with reserve trenches behind, and when one side attacked, the attack was on a front of so many miles. In the Spanish war attacks are made not on lines of trenches, but on definite positions such as a town or fortified ridge or hill or – more often – a group of farm buildings or houses. It is this which has made so much more destruction; it is fought in streets and houses as much as in the open country.

At five o'clock next morning a four-hour lorry drive over an impossible road brought us to our destination. I was reminded of our first action, from Chinchon. Once more the war became to me like a game of soldiers, only this time I enjoyed it. Worries about my haversack and anxiety to do the correct thing were absent. I derived a lot of pleasure out of my special position as 'runner'; it gave me an important position and made the game of soldiers more amusing. Spades and picks were given out to most of the men, and I was lucky in being without them. When I took a message somewhere I could park my haversack, blanket and gasmask. Jeans promised me I could get rid of my rifle and carry a revolver as soon as he could get hold of one for himself and one for me. That would have made everything quite perfect.

It was a lovely day and our high spirits of the night before continued. Joe and I were in quite an hysterical mood, roaring with laughter at each other's jokes. These were only somewhat laboured irony on the general inefficiency of everything. I felt this was going to be like our manoeuvres at the castle. I had thoroughly enjoyed those. Tanks and armoured cars passed us, and everything looked quite picturesque, including ourselves in single file.

Planning an attack, talking about the artillery and the infantry and the tanks, executing a flank movement, carrying dispatches, all these things are only a healthy out-door sport, and – if carried on without the public school idea of 'discipline' – a very pleasant one. That was how it was at the manoeuvres at the castle; that was how it was now.

If you do all the firing, all the attacking, all the shelling and bombing yourself, there is nothing to make you a pacifist. It is when you are part of an 'enemy concentration' being 'dispersed by artillery fire', when all the death in the form of high speed lead and scraps of jagged metal and high explosive is coming in your direction that you begin to understand what 'war' means.

You hear people say they are against war because they think killing is wrong. I have never been moved by the sight of our planes raining bombs on enemy troops or by the thought that I have perhaps scored a direct hit on a Moor. Joe and I and Tich and Babs and Ray and Messer all talked this out the night before all except two of us were killed. We all agreed in the end. The time you are a real pacifist is the time you know real sickening fear. That was as near as any of us got to being pacifists; the war in Spain, the war of modern death weapons, chosen by fascism, had to be fought and won. If you object to capitalist wars, you can show a set of well-founded principles for not wanting to fight in them. With us, who had chosen to fight, there was only one cause for disliking it – fear. Fortunately hardly anyone was afraid to admit his fear.

Fear took people in different ways. Some were affected by fear of machine-gun bullets; some by their own hand grenades; some by the ever constant threat of being surrounded and taken prisoner; some by the possibility of disablement and wounding; some by the fear of death. I did not mind bullets much, and I never thought of being captured. But waiting between the whine of shells falling near me made me sweat – not with nervous anticipation, not with excitement, or heat – but sweat with Fear.

✳

I was sent to find out where the battalion on our right was. Birch came with me. We saw a lorry just starting up, a quarter of a mile away, and signalled to it to wait for us. There were Frenchmen and Spaniards, mixed, belonging to the Marseillaise Battalion. They told us the way to find the positions was to come with them and see the commander.

'Can't you tell us where the lines are?' I asked.

But they would give us no information and were impatient to be off. The road wound round into a little village, which was our destination. Constant bombing was now going on, and every ten minutes the lorry would stop, and we would get off and lie in the ditch.

We arrived at what might have been the Town Hall. There were three floors, each filled in every space with men and their equipment. Some were eating, a few sleeping, most lay stretched out like tired dogs, with eyes wide open. They paid no attention to the shells. We went on to the 'front', barely half a kilometre down the road, past the church where a red flag flew from the steeple; the door and windows shielded machine-gunners behind hastily erected sand-bagged barricades. Bullets whistled near us; one spluttered against a still unbroken stained glass window. The 'front' was a semi-circular ridge, but we could see no one in firing position. A Spanish captain told us they had fought a rear-guard action all night. Their losses had been terrible. He pointed back to the village. 'In front of that road you have come along, there is nothing. . . . You should make a line to join up with us.'

Just then a shell crashed into a near-by dug-out and we ducked low. There was nothing more to say or do; we ran back to the village.

✳

The captain had left us. In the throng of men coming to and fro, and voices shouting in French and Spanish, we were quite lost. Everything seemed to be in a state of complete confusion. Every two or three minutes would come the familiar sound of a shrieking whistle followed by a crash as the rebels' shrapnel shells landed in the little village street. One room of the building had been turned into a temporary dressing-station, and from it came the groans of the wounded and dying. The bombardment was becoming more intensive, and I expected every moment that our building would be hit.

We stepped aside as two men passed with a blood-stained stretcher; their casualty had been hit through the head.

'What are you all doing here?' asked one of them. 'Why aren't you in position? There are barely a dozen men and only one machine-gun at the church!'

'You think the fascists are going to walk right into their own barrage? No, my friend, Dumont knows his business; time enough to reinforce the front line when the shelling stops.'

'For Christ's sake, come on,' Birch tugged at my elbow. 'We've no earthly reason for seeing Dumont again; we've got our information, so let's get back.'

I looked towards the window; getting back seemed none too healthy a proposition.

'It'll take us over an hour,' I said. 'Let's ask Dumont for transport.'

We went upstairs, had the same parleying with the guard, and found him. As Birch had remarked as we went up, our presence didn't seem to give him any particular joy. I told him we had seen their front line positions, asked again if he had any message, told him we would return, and was there any transport?

'You may find a lorry perhaps,' and that was that.

We stood at the door, waiting for a burst; then we went out. It was like going into a hurricane, never knowing when the fatal gust was coming. There was something indescribably sinister about the shriek and the burst and the cloud of smoke of the shrapnel in that dusty village street.

'We don't know the name of this village,' I said. 'I'll ask.'

The first man inside told me, but Spanish names spoken

by Spaniards sound almost incomprehensible to foreigners. There was a delay of three or four minutes while they looked for someone who could write; I spelled it out.

B o a d i l l a   d e l   M o n t e.

'Come on.' Birch was getting impatient; he told me he thought we should have been back before. The sound of the explosion of the guns wasn't so bad – you heard it in threes, wang, wang, wang, then the shrieks and bursts, one after the other. The third one – as we got to the top of the road – seemed meant for us, and we lay flat on our stomachs in the ditch. I thought it must be on top of us when we heard the burst; then, thirty seconds later, I realized something had hit my helmet. We stretched out our hands, picked up some of the wicked little bits of metal, and dropped them quickly; they were red hot.

'Come on, quick, before the battery gets going again.'

I suddenly thought how very pleasant it would be to go on lying on my stomach in this wet ditch.

'The only thing's to fall flat on your stomach when this shrapnel starts,' said Birch. 'Perhaps we ought to set them an example by showing we aren't afraid; if we run, it looks as if we're running away.'

I didn't care what 'they' thought, and for that matter no one could see us now. The next three shells burst behind us, and we thought we were out of their range at last. But it is a curious thing that when you retire from shell-fire, the shells always seem to follow you. In another minute we were on our stomachs again. I was already hot and tired. My mess tin had come unstrapped from the belt, and was dangling all over the place; my gasmask kept hitting me in the chest when I ran; when I fell on my stomach half the ammunition fell out of my pouches. That was a bad morning. Finally I threw the mess tin away.

We walked as briskly as possible along the road. We had made up our minds that there wasn't any transport, and there wasn't. It was a relief to be out of the shelling; it had given me almost the most nasty feeling in my stomach I have ever had. As we turned a corner in the road, there was another familiar sound – swish, swish, swish, swish, swish.

My first feeling was simply one of annoyance; there must be some mistake; they couldn't be shelling from one side, and machine-gunning the road from the other!

There was no lower ground we could get on to, so we had to go into the woods and dodge from tree to tree. It was getting very warm.

I suppose there had been aeroplanes flying about all the morning; the noise of their engines wasn't noticed by us as we'd missed the familiar *'Fliege, Decke!'* shouts. Now it seemed suddenly they were everywhere in the sky. Three, six, nine, twelve fascist light bombers, and far up above them we could see the escort fighters. The drone of their engines faded in the distance. Then, quite suddenly, we saw three heavy Junkers. They were coming right over us, then they circled half-left and bombed the village, circled away, returned and dropped another load. We could not see where the bombs had dropped, but we saw thick clouds of smoke. Now there were six fascist planes circling round and round at the rear of the Thaelmann position – looking for the artillery, we guessed.

In a clearing on the road we saw five tanks, heavy ones with pom-pom guns. They were being hastily camouflaged with branches of trees; but three aeroplanes circled low overhead, and then disappeared over the enemy lines. There was not one Government plane to be seen.

This time we recognized the noise – these were three-engined Junkers approaching. We ran as fast as we could away from the tanks, and tumbled into a dug-out where some of the Spanish troops were making a meal of bread and Russian meat. The planes didn't worry them at all. They got up and shook their fists at them.

There were six machines; most of their bombs fell near us, covering us with dirt. None of the tanks were hit. We got up and went on.

Running and walking alternately for another ten minutes,

I began to feel the sweat trickling down under my three sweaters. There wasn't any danger now, just annoyance because it was taking so long running about to find our zug. Then we saw Arnold. We hadn't missed much, because they had spent the time digging and no one seemed to have enjoyed it much. Joe had been carrying my blanket and haversack. His face was very red: he was by himself, eating out of a tin of corned beef. Birch and I settled down with Jeans and began to give hurried and breathless explanations.

'Draw a map, can't you, just a sketch?' he asked.

I tried to draw in the village, the road that curved round into it, the church, the front line positions.

'Which is north?'

I hadn't the slightest idea. Birch took the paper and drew a new map. It seemed I was all wrong in my sense of direction. I was sure he was right (which, indeed, he was), I hadn't noticed the curves in the road.

'Well, you'd better go now and take it back to Walter and explain it,' said Arnold. 'Have a rest afterwards.'

'Where is he?'

'Back on the road behind.' I sighed as I picked myself and all my equipment up (my trousers as usual slipping down), and began to lumber off. But I was quite impressed with the importance of it all, and meant to try and render in German a vivid description of our trip to Boadilla.

Walter and Herbert were standing under a tree, Walter looking at something with his field-glasses. I gave him the map, and explained that there was no one between us and Dumont's battalion. Herbert told me there were a lot of troops in front of us, and this was only a reserve position.

'Shall I go back?' I asked.

'No, stay here till there are the orders to take.'

I lay down, prepared for a good rest, but it was no good, as Herbert and Walter kept walking off somewhere else and I had to be near them. Lorries were constantly coming along with a few people wrapped in blankets; I could see they weren't ours but belonged to a Spanish column. There were a lot of Spaniards about all the time, but I couldn't make out where they came from. Walter was talking in Spanish to a man about the revolver he was carrying; the man produced a paper, a permit to own this from the Socialist Party.

Walter wrote something on it, then the man gave him the revolver and went off. Later on Arnold arrived and was handed the revolver. He was very pleased about it. Soon it was clear that a Spanish column ahead of us was retiring.

Messer arrived on another food lorry. I was glad to see him, and Jeans also greeted him heartily. I asked him all about his stay in Madrid when he had left the hospital. While we talked, bombing and reconnoitring by enemy planes was in progress, and the three of us crouched under a tree.

About twenty minutes later shells began to hit the road. Ahead of us was the noise of rifle and machine-gun fire, but the thickness of the trees made it impossible to see anything. We saw only an occasional flash from the fascists' artillery; it seemed to be this side of their ridge. The firing was going on between their ridge and ours, where the country was a succession of woody rises gradually getting lower from each side till they met in a valley in the middle. Walter had field-glasses, and Arnold told us they could see large numbers of the enemy descending the slopes. Behind their ridge was the road from Navalcarnero to the University City.

Birch and I were told to go forward and find out where were the advance lines of the Spanish troops and what was happening. We went cautiously as the sound of firing grew nearer, hopping from tree to tree. On the way we passed men coming back supporting wounded comrades. They had none of our heavy equipment, only a rifle, bandoliers of ammunition slung over their shoulders and most of them a scarf or hat in the black and red colours of the anarchists.

'What's happening?' I asked one of them in French. Then Birch tried Spanish. The man shrugged his shoulders, spoke very fast, and went on. Then I found a boy wandering about with no immediate aim in view apparently, and he promised to take us to the front line positions.

'It is dangerous,' he said. 'Be careful; the enemy may see us. Just now four of their tanks came over. It is terrible, the line is breaking.'

We came in sight of a lane along the bottom of the valley, and I could see we were barely half a mile from the church of Boadilla. In the road were three lorries and an ambulance. As we reached it, the gravel a few feet away crumpled apart. We lay flat down in the ditch the other side. While I counted sixty the lane was infiltrated with machine-gun bullets.

Someone waved to us from behind a tree up the bank. 'Don't stay there! You can be seen!' he shouted. 'Come up here.'

He was a Frenchman, attached to the Red Cross. He asked if the road to Boadilla was safe. Twenty yards from where we had crossed, it curved round out of the range of the enemy's machine-guns, but he thought the fascists might have entered the village. I said I didn't think this was so, as we had been there this morning. He told us the front lines had retreated, that the tanks had killed many men, that there were now no proper lines at all, the casualties had been heavy, some of the Columna Libra had gone right back in the centre (these must have been those people we had seen back with Walter and our lorries), others had tried to get to Boadilla.

Birch was impatient. 'What we've got to do is to find out where the front positions are, and go back and report; you don't want to go on discussing what this man thinks ought to have been done,' he said.

We crouched lower as a few bullets sped overhead, then I answered: 'You don't understand him. He's saying there aren't any lines and telling what's happened.'

The Red Cross man went on to say that, having nothing to meet the tanks with, the troops were demoralized.

'Ask him where the front is,' said Birch. I asked him.

He told us there were about a hundred people a little way ahead, behind the various trees. While we waited, we could see this number diminish.

176

Men came back singly. Then came four, carrying a blanket with a dead man in it; then one with two of his fingers shot off; then three together. At the edge of the road they paused, then dashed across. The Frenchman shouted to a wounded man asking if he wanted any help; he shook his head and limped on. When the four with the blanket crossed, we heard the vicious tearing of the blanket as bullets riddled its load. They dropped it in the middle. The dead man fell for a second to a sitting position. His body met a hurricane of lead; as he rolled flat on to the ground he was in two pieces.

We returned, keeping nearer to the village on the way back. I told the boy who had brought us, and who was lying behind a tree a few yards away, that several battalions of the International Brigade were behind. I thought the news might cheer him, as he seemed very depressed.

Having got past the danger zone in silence we argued for the rest of the way. Birch said our job was to report where the front was, and it was not our job to talk about morale.

Soon – as I had expected – came the order for the Thaelmann Battalion to advance. I had to keep liaison between the three zugs. This was easy until we came under fire. Then I made a vital mistake. I had thought we would be going over the same ground that Birch and I had already covered; actually we took a direction almost forty-five degrees to the left, away from Boadilla. I found the first zug, and the light machine-gun zug, and by this time running about was an uncomfortable business; everyone was crouching behind trees. I dashed to another tree where two men were lying in firing position, and threw myself down beside them. Bullets came unpleasantly close. The tree was not thick enough to shelter three of us.

'Who are you? Are you from the 2nd Zug?'

Neither of them answered.

I shouted: 'Are you 2nd Zug?'

Bullets twanged through the branches of the tree above our heads. It was a rotten position altogether, as a piece of rising ground ahead prevented any view. They were too preoccupied with the bullets to answer.

I cursed them, and went on saying '2nd Zug'. Then one pointed to the left. I gathered these were people from the machine-gun section who had got separated; now I recognized them as being among the new lot that had arrived from Albacete at El Prado a week before. It was their first time under fire.

I went on towards what I imagined to be the extreme left wing. Soon I was following a track in the valley, and the sounds of battle grew more distant. Now I could hear only the pounding of heavy guns in the distance. Everything was curiously peaceful; I might have been going for a walk in the woods in England. I had time to realize how lovely the country was – and ten minutes before I had had to lie behind a tree with someone pouring lead in my direction. There seemed a very big gap in the lines, and I decided to return. Like so many actions in this war, this one was evidently taking place on a very small front – probably the only objective of the rebels' attack was Boadilla.

Suddenly I heard a single rifle shot. I have found that to hear the explosion in a rifle barrel never gives one the slightest cause for alarm. I suppose instinctively one feels if you can hear it so near it cannot be the enemy's, where as when I hear the sound of a bullet travelling I am inclined at once to get the protection of earth or trees in front of me.

I listened carefully, and hearing nothing more, shouted: '1st Company, 2nd Zug! 1st Company! 2nd Zug.'

A few hundred yards in the direction I had been taking, five figures emerged on to the path and ran fast away, keeping to the side. They disappeared from view and a few bullets passed near me. I did not wait for any more. I ran as fast as I could back the way I had come, keeping to the path all the way so as not to lose direction.

When I found Jeans once more, the whole company had taken up positions on a ridge overlooking the lane where Birch and I had seen the lorries and the ambulance. I had wandered too much over to the left, where there was no

fighting, our troops being established in positions two kilometres back. For us the whole Boadilla sector was a salient.

There was continual firing and machine-guns were in
action on both sides. I was allowed to have a rest, which
I badly needed. First I had to give myself the pleasure of
describing my adventures graphically to Jeans, and then to
Joe.

'You've missed something here, boy!' Joe told me. 'We've
been potting them properly; see 'em plain as anything. Some
b— says don't fire, it's too far; don't you believe it. I've seen
'em drop.'

We were both sitting twenty yards from the top of the
ridge, fairly secure from fire. People were taking it in turns
to go and take up positions right at the top, where they
could sometimes see the enemy on the opposite ridge.

'Ay, did you see that?' shouted Jock. 'Lorrie and I saw
them drop, I tell ye.'

In the valley behind us a staff conference was going on,
with Rickard, Herbert, Jeans, and the other zug commanders.
Jeans called me, and Herbert gave a message for me to
deliver to Walter.

'You will find him with Commandant Dumont,'* he said.

'In the village?'

'No, I don't think he's as far. If you follow our line to
the right that takes you to the village, but you will see him
on the way, I expect.'

I walked along the ridge where he had shown me the way.
Next to the Thaelmann was the Edgar André Battalion,
then I saw some men of the Franco-Spanish lot; I was sure
they were the same I had seen in Boadilla that morning.
They were on the road, a few hundred yards behind. We
were no more than a quarter of a mile from Boadilla. I went
back and asked: 'Where is Commandant Dumont?'

* Major Dumont, an ex-French regular officer who now commanded the Commune de Paris battalion, a part of the XIth International Brigade, and the main French group in the Republican
Army.

179

A man pointed in the direction I had come from.

'He is not in Boadilla, in the village?' I asked in surprise, and received the no less surprising reply:

'The enemy is in Boadilla.'

Just at that moment a battery of four guns started up from behind the enemies' lines. It was nearly half-past five. The men huddled together round a lorry where wounded men lay groaning under blankets. The cold wind that had sprung up suddenly, the loss of Boadilla, the wounded men, the shells hurtling overhead, all these things suited each other; all made a depressing picture. I experienced once more the same feeling of physical and moral dejection I had had when we had carried dead men back on stretchers in the cold night drizzle from the Casa Velasquez.

He was wrong. The enemy were not in Boadilla then. Four hours later we heard from the village the noise of wild shouting and screams; the shouts – with the occasional explosion of a rifle – went on all night. Boadilla had been almost surrounded, with the road to the rear under machine-gun fire. Evacuation had been quick and sudden. Fourteen wounded men in an improvised dressing-station were among what had been left behind. Those wild screams might be theirs – mingled with the shouts of the Moors who occupied the village.

There was only an occasional strafing over our heads that night. Joe and I shared the shelter of a thick pine tree for our rest periods; three people were on guard at a time, the sentries' positions being on a ridge ahead. This was on lower ground than the one where the main body was established, and nothing much could be seen.

The next morning we hoped we would counter-attack and re-take the village. As a rule, one's spirits are always high on the second day of an action; and there had been few casualties the day before. We thought Boadilla should never have been lost, and the story of the wounded men was a rumour and probably exaggerated. But we took part in no action for the next three days. On the first day we dug sporadically, and there were a few reconnoitring parties.

The second day was devoted to more serious and organized construction of proper dug-outs. One the third, we embarked on a communication trench, to join up the dug-outs behind every tree, and make a complete 'line' of the whole battalion. The trench was never completed properly, and if you had to move about whilst a 'strafing' was going on, it was safest to crawl on your stomach.

A thick mist made it possible to dig in comparative safety. A manifesto was read to us from the Spanish High Command which referred to the dislike of the principle of digging in by the militia. It suggested three possible reasons – 'excessive courage, carelessness, downright laziness'. In my case certainly, the last was the correct reason. When Joe and I had completed our dug-out and made it warm and comfortable, I envisaged a very pleasant time ahead, reading, smoking, eating, drinking, occasionally cleaning my rifle, and sleeping. These ideas were rudely shattered by the order to dig a communication trench. There were at least twenty yards between Joe and myself and the next tree on the left which sheltered a dug-out with three Germans and the light machine-gun. I knew Joe would make sure we did not do an overshare of the digging. On our right Birch was by himself, then Jock and Messer were together, then Sid, then Tich and Babs and Ray and Jeans in one big dug-out, then Aussie, and on his right, behind the road, the beginning of the Edgar André Battalion.

There was plenty of food, wine and cognac, and apart from the digging, we had quite a pleasant time. I can remember nearly every detail of this period at the front, and easily imagine myself reliving it. One or two incidents stand out. Once when Joe and I went together to draw the rations for the zug in the evening, we were stranded with a heavy coffee container on a piece of rising ground just when the lines flared up into fire on both sides; two bullets in rapid succession hit the pot, and Joe's hand was scalded by the hot liquid.

These sudden bursts of firing were caused by patrols.

Sometimes, after a quarter of an hour of it, one would find one had been firing at one's own people returning.

'Don't shoot. Patrol out,' would be shouted, but somehow the order would get lost and everyone would join in. Even the sentries returning from the ridge ahead sometimes provoked an outburst of fire. Once the guards saw men digging in on a ridge opposite, a good way to the left, away from the village. This we were told, was the left wing of the Thaelmann Battalion. Later on, it turned out it was the enemy. At the end of three days, we were securely established with little more than half a mile between us and the enemy.

While Babs was on guard with two Germans, they observed sixteen men creeping on their stomachs towards our lines. They passed near without seeing the guards. Babs joined up behind the last one, so when they arrived there were seventeen. Fortunately the sixteen in front also turned out to be our own people.

For me the most important incident was when someone called my name, and I saw John Cornford with his head bandaged. He was probably the first Englishman to enlist in the war, as before joining the International Brigade he had fought with a Spanish column at Huesca.* Then he went back to England at the end of August, and returned with seven other Englishmen who were part of the Marseillaise Battalion. So at last we had found the 'other English lot'. They had had a number of casualties at the University City, and had occupied the big red building at the same time as we were at the Casa Velasquez. They were at Boadilla with Dumont's brigade, as a machine-gun team. On the day of its capture, they had been keeping up a continual fire from the church. At four o'clock one of them had gone back for fresh orders to the village, just in time to see the last troops leaving; it was almost evacuated behind them. Their two machine-guns were the last to leave Boadilla, and they left

* Cornford was not quite the first Englishman to enlist. That distinction was the achievement of two East End 'garment-workers' Sam Masters and Nat Cohen.

two of their number dead behind them. Now they were in reserve, behind the Thaelmann and Edgar André Battalions.

John Cornford – like Arnold Jeans and Lorrimer Birch – fitted into my category of Real Communists. He was killed in the first week of January, with the British Battalion at Cordoba.

On the third day a German attached to the staff showed me the whole line. For nearly a mile a rough communication trench connected dug-outs on a ridge; then the ground sloped downwards to a valley – this was unoccupied. Half a mile to the left, four machine-guns on a hill commanded this valley, then our lines went back, for the machine-guns faced east as well as south. On the other side, beyond Boadilla, our lines went fairly straight for five miles before going back.

At five o'clock the mist lifted. Six Russian fighting planes crossed our lines, and dived low over the enemy; three times they went over, their machine-guns spraying the positions. An attack was expected through the valley which divided our lines. Everyone stood ready, but there was nothing save desultory shelling on both sides.

While I was seeing the lines, a young man in a thick blue sweater – a Spaniard – asked where each battalion was. He wanted to know whether the Thaelmann and Edgar André Battalions were in the sector, and whether there were only troops of the International Brigade. He had come from a Spanish column on the other side of Boadilla, he said. He got some information, then said he would go on to see another zug commander. In the failing light his figure could just be seen crossing the deserted valley.

'Hi! Hullo-o-o-o! Hey, there! Not that way!'

The shouts produced no effect, the stranger ran on. Now we began to think of the circumstances of his arrival, who he might be. A sinister word was whispered: 'Spy!' Diffidently at first, then with growing momentum. A blaze of fire started from the Thaelmann Battalion. Two machine-guns opened up, pouring lead into the valley. But the last anyone saw of the stranger was a speck disappearing into the darkness.

*

Joe had been back to Majadahonda to fetch our packs. He returned about seven o'clock.

'I could have stayed over till tomorrow, only I thought that was a bit thick, spending the night back, now we're so short here,' he said.

I was glad he had returned, and went on with some of the digging. I had had neuralgia all day, and bending down caused acute stabs of pain in my forehead.

'You lie down and take a good rest, boy,' said Joe. 'Let some of these Fritzies get on with the job.' Our communication trench was nothing like properly completed.

No one slept much that night. A patrol of twenty-three men with a Lewis gun under Walter had gone out, and we waited anxiously for its return. They aimed to hold up an enemy car on the road the other side of Boadilla, capture the inmates, and get vital information.

The patrol came back at five o'clock the next morning. All night there was constant noise from the fascists' lines – noise of heavy traffic. After a little we could distinguish the various sounds – tanks, troop lorries, mules dragging heavy guns. No one doubted what this noise meant. Tomorrow the enemy would attack.

Knowing this, we were impatient. The ceaseless steady rumble a mile away jarred on our nerves. Why was nothing done now, to forestall the attack?

By now our dug-outs were comfortable. We sat and talked and smoked cigarettes (carefully shielded behind the parapet) and munched and sipped wine or coffee. I felt wide awake. Soon we stopped discussing the attack and the efficiency of the command.

Tich talked more about the business he and Babs had had in Dover. Before the night was over, they had agreed to start another business in London with Ray and Jeans as partners. Arnold said he hoped the immigration authorities would be kinder this time.

Jock and Messer were arguing as usual, and even Sid – after heavy cursing – was allowed to join in.

Joe and Birch and I were on guard together. In the last two days another change had come over Birch. Previously he had thought Joe was always trying to get the better of him and make a fool of him. Now at last Joe's patent good nature had had its effect. As for me, I began to feel almost as friendly with Birch as I had been at Albacete. He told us how sick he had felt to see people deserting and not wanting to fight, and only thinking of being relieved; how during the castle episode he had wanted to join a different group of the German Battalion and not to be associated with the English. But after a few hours' argument, he admitted he had been over-critical in his judgments.

I thought about Birch all the time I had known him – how at Albacete he had been friendly and helpful and hearty; I remembered how we had visited a brothel and subscribed for Sid's pleasure; how he had been humorous even in his perpetual duel with Keith; then I remembered how much I had liked him at Chinchon after the first action; then next the triangular row with him and Messer when we had carried Alex's dead body from the White House; then all the time we had been into Madrid as close friends, and how I had persuaded him to meet and tolerate Watson again; then the quarrel over the anti-tank squad the second time we were at the White House, and how amazing it was to hear Birch being cynical about everything for the first time; then the time at the Playa when Birch was drunk and rude the whole time and thought everyone was trying to do him down – and how one evening Jeans told me all about how he had been at Barcelona in the Centuria; the feud Birch had had with Joe and Aussie and me at the castle.

Then I remembered all about Joe – how I had started by rather apprehensive laughter which soon changed to positive dislike of him all the time we were at Chinchon; then how I had begun to like him in Madrid and the second time at the White House, and then how we had shared everything at the Playa and become very close friends all the time from then.

Well now, the Birch and Joe feud was over. I was glad.

185

Joe produced a thermos he had 'organized' at Majadahonda, and we had some coffee and some of his private store of brandy.

'Better keep some of this till tomorrow, might need it, boy. Good night.'

'Good night.'

Chapter 14

My neuralgia was worse in the morning – it hurt to get up. Jeans told us we were all to get ready with rifles loaded. 'It's almost certain the attack'll be soon,' he said.

It was half-past seven. After waiting ten minutes we began to eat the rations they had brought up. 'You lie down there, quiet, boy,' said Joe. 'I'll see if I can get a spot of brandy we can fill up with.'

Food made me feel better, but I still blinked wearily – our trench seemed to have the appearance of a party the morning after. The little Austrian doctor came up to see if there were any cases for treatment. Jeans brought him along to our dug-out. The doctor gave me two aspirins which I swallowed with the brandy. Jeans asked me if I was all right, or if I wanted to go back. I was all right.

We could hear the rumble of tanks and lorries from the enemies' lines even more clearly than in the night. The big guns had started up on both sides, but that meant nothing much. At ten o'clock there was a nasty rush of short range rifle fire. I crept on my stomach back to our dug-out. We crouched down.

'Don't like those bullets, boy,' said Joe. 'You keep your head down. Did you see that one, slap into that tree there, might have got my fingers; sounds like something wrong this time of the morning.'

Jeans was walking along the ridge behind us with Walter and the doctor.

'That fellow's a bloomin' marvel; can't keep his head down. They'll get him one day.'

We heard shouting on our right, and I peered cautiously up to see what was happening. The doctor was bending down on his knees, someone was hit. Jock had a bullet through the side of his neck. When the strafing ceased a minute, two stretcher-bearers ran up from the valley behind and took him back.

I heard Babs say: 'I thought Jock was shamming at first. You know he's always up to that sort of thing, so when I saw him lying on the ground I didn't take any notice.'

Birch shouted: 'There's a fascist sniper on that first ridge there. They couldn't have got Jock otherwise.'

All of this is very clear. Jock being wounded, Jock being taken back, Birch talking about the sniper and cursing Sid. All these things belong to another existence – they happened before that orderly life of ours which I regarded as everlasting because it was so strongly present, before that finished.

This was a big attack. We had our positions; we were well entrenched; we knew where our lines were; we knew we were on one ridge, the enemy on another; we knew all about the whole point of the fascist attack – to cut the Escorial road and encircle Madrid to the north. So it ought to have been simple – something of which you can give a thrilling dramatic description. How we withstood the shells and the bombs and the swooping aeroplanes and the fire of machine-gun and rifle, how we held our positions against bombs and hand grenades, how we fixed our bayonets as they charged our lines, withdrew and disputed the ground, inch by inch, hand to hand. . . . But that sort of thing only happens in fiction and journalism.

A few minutes after Jock went back, our dug-outs were crowded with Spaniards. I don't know how they got there, probably they came up from behind, then over the top. I don't know whether the bullets were still twanging through the branches when they arrived – I am sure we did not fire. Practically all that morning, we still had the command: 'Don't shoot. Patrol out.' The patrol had returned long ago, but we were good at obeying orders.

The Spaniards talked about tanks and about their bombs being no good. They crowded the dug-outs and the shallow communication trenches – there was no room to move. Joe and I had five in our dug-out. There is only one word for their state, they were scared stiff. Perhaps if we had understood them their fear would have communicated itself to us. It didn't. We cheered them up; we pointed out how good the trench was; we stammered slogans about camaradas; we offered them sardines. Joe and Birch were the best at this. After five minutes the men who had been forced in, quivering, at the pistol point, were pulling out red scarfs and handkerchiefs and shouting, '*Viva la Brigada Internationala!*'

'What's happening?' I shouted to Birch.

'It's obvious,' he shouted back, over the heads of five Spaniards (I was pleased and relieved, I knew Birch would know, would find it obvious). 'These chaps have all been in the trenches over the ridge on our right, towards Boadilla, God knows who's there now. Where's Jeans? We can't all stay here in this trench, a shell in here will blow us all out of it. Hi, Tich, you're in command now. Couldn't we get these chaps digging while there's time?'

'We'll have to wait till Jeans comes back with the orders.'

I slipped out and ran along the ridge to the left to see if the Germans in our zug and the other zugs further to the left were still there, and if there were any messages. The machine-gunners next to us were worried – there was no news. Then I saw Jeans panting up the ridge and I went back to see him.

'Thaelmann Battalion forward to the right!'

They were shuffling and scrambling along before we got the message. I shouted it back to the Germans on our left. 'Thaelmann, everyone!'

Joe shouted with me. Bullets were singing over the trench, but the fire was not very intense. Everyone was getting back from the dug-outs to the lower ground behind – the men in front seemed to be going along straight, parallel with the ridge. It looked like a disorganized retreat.

'We're going to advance,' I shouted to the Spaniards. Birch could speak Spanish better, he seized one of them by the shoulder to explain. This one produced a pole with a black and red flag which he waved in the air, the rest grouped round him. The confusion was the beginning of the tragedy; some wanted to come with us in an attack, others thought we were retreating and leaving them to hold the position alone – they wanted to come with us too. As Joe and I scrambled off to catch up the rest of the English we turned back and shouted once again for the Germans to follow us. Some of the Spaniards came, but the whole of the first and second zugs on our left stayed in their trenches – they had received new orders. We ran along the edge of the ridge and I passed Aussie. He was sitting down pulling up his boots.

'Come on, Aussie,' Joe shouted. 'You'll miss this if you don't hurry!'

All the English were together – we were separated from the rest. Jeans was in front with Tich and Birch close behind him, Babs was close to Sid, then Joe and I, who had decided to keep together whatever happened, and Ray Cox behind us – we were a solid mass. I had no idea where we were going or what was happening. I don't think we went along for more than five minutes, just beyond the protection of the ridge to the right, when we had to stop and lie down on account of the hail of bullets that came over.

'I don't know where Oswald is,' I heard Jeans saying. 'He must be ahead of us somewhere, with a whole patrol. Where are the other zugs?'

All this is still quite clear – I can picture it today. We sat and lay on the grass slope, or crouched behind the trees; we talked about what was happening. It might have been a Group Meeting.

The bullets were getting unpleasant. They were coming from the ridge the Spaniards had evacuated – that must be it; if we kept behind the trees, we were safe. We returned the fire.

*

Then Tich and Birch were leaning over Jeans's body.

'We can't do anything,' I heard someone say, and then, 'We've got to get him out here, you pull his feet down, Lorrie, I'll get hold of the head.'

I sat up and saw Jeans's face under a pool of blood. They were trying to get his helmet off. 'Cut the strap, Lorrie, with your bayonet,' I heard. It was Tich, groping over to hold up the chin of the man lying still on the grass. 'That bullet must have come from the left, where our own trenches are; we're under cross fire.'

At this moment we all had to duck flat as another hurricane of lead came over.

When I looked up and spoke to Joe I turned my head. That was just incidental – it wasn't because he had not answered. Joe was kneeling on the grass, his gun pointed on to the ground through his hands. I could touch him with my arm. I tried not to look at his head – it was sunk forward on to his chest. I felt I was in the presence of something horrifying. I didn't think about where we were, or the bullets – I didn't think about Joe being dead – I just thought it was all wrong Joe's head being like that. I picked it up. Then there were more bullets, and I lay flat again – that was instinctive. Perhaps I was there three minutes.

Tich and Birch were still arguing about Jeans. I heard someone say, 'He's finished,' but all the time I was quite calm. I kept saying to myself, 'All right, Joe's killed, that's finished, absolutely settled, that's all right, Joe's killed, that's the end of that,' till the words screamed in my ears. All that is still clear. Afterwards it is not so plain.

Tich was shouting out: 'Get back, all of you, quick as you can,' and Ray was sitting in front of a tree firing when he crumpled up and collapsed. These are blurred images. Then my own name being called, 'Here, Romilly, here, quick, man, run all out,' and I rushed through a hail of bullets to a bank where Babs was lying. After that we were together all the time. I went on saying, 'I must find Walter and tell him Joe is dead.' We saw men pouring across the ridge behind us. We were safe where we were; and I climbed up a tree to see over the valley – it was better than the maddening suspense of waiting. Through the branches I saw silvery gleams moving up the track. I knew they were tanks, but it wasn't very real. And later on we ran back till we had to throw ourselves down on the grass and rest. All this is very blurred. Only Joe's head, slumped forward, was real, and Babs shouting to me to run quickly.

Then there were forty of us (this is only a number we thought of afterwards), Germans and Spaniards, mixed up together. We were firing all the time. I copied the others and fired in the same direction till the barrel was red-hot. And always, starting every few minutes, there was the deadly cross fire. But we were in woods now and the trees were thicker, and we would wait behind a thick one, then dodge back quickly to the next tree behind. There are some things which stand out clearer – the sun getting hotter, and stumbling over belts and coats and ammunition discarded in the retreat, and the lack of any feeling when someone fell, only the quick rush back to the next tree.

And then the blur was over, and everything was quiet all around, and we gathered together; and this time I counted and there were seventeen of us, and a few people were talking and arguing, but most were just resting. I didn't think about Joe then, I wanted to sleep and forget everything.

It was cooling and growing dark when we found the rest of our company – Aussie was there, and he told me, 'When I'd got my boots on, you were all gone, and the Spaniards only waited a couple of minutes and they were off. There's a lot of wounded men they left there in the trench. Next thing, I was standing down below when I saw them fellows come over the parapet – walking ever so steadily, and they were calling out, 'Don't fire, comrades.' So I hung around as I thought these were the same bunch – and I heard a lot of shooting going on, so I looked up again and I saw these fellows. I couldn't make out any sort of uniform or what they were, but they weren't Moors, I'll swear that, Spaniards they must have been, they were strolling along that trench with their guns on to the ground, firing – took no notice of anything, you know, just took it all calmly, finishing them off. There was a whole cluster of us down in the valley there, some of that bunch of anarchists were still hanging about and waiting around to see what was happening and old Harry was there, so we started letting 'em have it. Took 'em by surprise all right at first. There's one big fellow – I know I got him all right. Next moment all our bunch was gone, so I followed as quick as I could. It seemed all quiet, and someone shouted *"Alto! Alto!"* and I got behind a tree and saw two of these chaps calling out, so I put my gun up to fire and a took a shot, but it didn't get him, and I took another, then he said comrades. But I knew they weren't our lot, they'd got a green uniform on and red caps like the Moors. So I took another shot and got one of 'em and the other one dashed off, and I didn't wait any longer. Then I came up with the Germans, and Sid was in their bunch and Birch, too. Sid was on the ground with a bullet in his stomach. He was dead – right dead – when I got there, and one of the Germans told me he said to give his salutations to the English comrades. I never saw Birch after that – I called out to him and he didn't hear, just went on you know, we were all firing, too, so it was the noise, and then I never saw him. Then Messer too. You know, when you passed me, Romilly, I was getting my boots on and I saw Messer then, he was getting a strap together on his pack, and that's all I saw of him.'

There were bombing-planes over us and shrapnel bursting behind – but all those were only incidents. At six o'clock the retreat stopped – Walter and Babs and the big fat English doctor, whom we had seen at Majadahonda, and who appeared without his coat, his arm grazed and bleeding, with a revolver in his hand, got most of the credit. The frantic rush from ridge to ridge, the frantic wild firing into the air, the frantic rush to go faster than those tanks was ended. Companies and groups and nationalities were all mixed up, but order ensued at last. I had a group of five Spaniards to command and place in positions on an advanced ridge, part of forty men whom Babs was given to cover the retreat of the main body while they re-organized and dug new trenches. There were incidents then – the sixty seconds when we saw a valley track filled with columns of men with brown skins and red caps, swinging along easily, carelessly, and we saw those ranks crumple up and scatter to the sides under our fire.

The battle went on three days. The enemy retreated finally till they occupied only our own original positions. The woods and slopes were covered with bodies and rifles and ammunition pouches. There were night patrols to recover rifles and ammunition and the bodies of our dead. None of the English could be found. But none of those last five days before we were relieved have much to do with this story.

The last chapter of our story was written on the day that Joe was killed. It was written when a dispirited little band gathered together that night – Babs and Aussie and I dug ourselves only a shallow protection – we had not much interest in parapets and firing positions. There was a thin, greasy soup and tepid cocoa. Walter took the roll-call of the 1st Company, Thaelmann Battalion, just before the midnight guard.

He called out each name and paused, till the suspense was unbearable. Oswald and his patrol of fifteen men were every one of them missing – and we thought of the rifles pointed downwards in that trench and the bayonet slashes in the bodies of the men they brought back. The commander crossed their names all with the same word:

'*Gefallen.*'

From the 1st and 2nd Zugs, fifteen men called out the answer, '*Hier!*' Forty-three did not answer.

'Third Zug.' Three Germans answered '*Hier*' before he came to the English Group.

Addley — no answer, no information,   '*gefallen*'.

Avener	—	killed,	*'gefallen'*.
Birch	—	no answer, believed killed,	*'gefallen'*.
Cox	—	killed,	*'gefallen'*.

The suspense was still there; we knew they were killed, but yet we did not believe it. It was as if this was their last chance to plead before the final death sentence of the word written against their names.

Gillan	—	wounded.	
Gough	—	killed,	*'gefallen'*.
Jeans	—	killed,	*'gefallen'*.
Messer	—	no answer, missing,	*'gefallen'*.

There had been nothing to break the chain of those answers – we were all at the end of the alphabet.

※

Those last five days at the front were not so bad. We had enough to think about in the cold, miserable damp and in the fighting that went on. It was the relief, the return to the castle of El Pardo that was bad.* They talked about the action, about what ought to have been done, about the men who had been killed.

There were speeches when we said good-bye to return to Albacete, Valencia, Barcelona and England. Commander Richard said: 'In the battles of the future, if we know that there are Englishmen on our left flank, or Englishmen on our right, then we shall know that we need give no thought nor worry to those positions.'†

We returned to England on January 3. Albacete was just the same, except that it was muddier and dirtier – and the troops now slept on the stone floors without mattresses. Here the first British battalion was being trained. It was part of

* After 1939 the Madrid residence of General Franco.

† Colonel 'Richard' was a German communist named Staimer. He survived both the civil war and the world war to become police chief in East Germany.

the section of a thousand Englishmen who, in February, were to hold the most vital positions near the Valencia road under twelve days of the biggest artillery bombardment of the war, then counter-attack and make Madrid's road safe for months – perhaps for good. I might have gone back and joined those men, who are the real heroes of the Spanish struggle. But I did not go. I got married and lived happily instead.

✻

Yet more and more I see that those three months were not just an adventure, an interlude. The mark which they left is something that does not diminish but grows with time. When we were all together at the castle of El Pardo there was a kind of faith which made us feel that we could not ever be destroyed. But seven of those men – including Joe – were killed at Boadilla. They were killed, and forgotten, because they were only important for a day. Then there were other fighters, other martyrs, other sympathies.

There is something frightening, something shocking about the way the world does not stop because those men are dead. Over all this war there is that feeling. It is not something which is specifically due to the fact that one is seeing the struggle of a race of people one loves, that one's friends are fighting, or have died – it is a feeling of the vastness of the thing which has caught up so many separate entities and individualities.

I am not a pacifist, though I wish it were possible to lead one's life without the intrusion of this ugly monster of force and killing – war – and its preparation. And it is not with the happiness of the convinced communist, but reluctantly that I realize that there will never be peace or any of the things I like and want, until that mixture of profit-seeking, self-interest, cheap emotion and organized brutality which is called fascism has been fought and destroyed for ever.